D1043268

THE SURVIVAL GUIDE FOR

Kids with LD*

*Learning Differences

Revised
& Updated
3rd Edition

Rhoda Cummings, Ed.D.

RIVERHEAD FREE LIBRARY
330 COURT STREET
RIVERHEAD, NEW YORK 11901

free spirit
PUBLISHING®

Text copyright © 2016 by Rhoda Cummings, Ed.D., and 2002, 1990 by Gary Fisher, Ph.D., and
Rhoda Cummings, Ed.D.
Illustrations copyright © 2016 by Free Spirit Publishing Inc.

All rights reserved under International and Pan-American Copyright Conventions. Unless otherwise noted, no part of this book may be reproduced, stored in a retrieval system, or transmitted in
any form or by any means, electronic, mechanical, photocopying, recording, or otherwise, without
express written permission of the publisher, except for brief quotations or critical reviews. For
more information, go to www.freespirit.com/permissions.

Free Spirit, Free Spirit Publishing, and associated logos are trademarks and/or registered trademarks of Free Spirit Publishing Inc. A complete listing of our logos and trademarks is available at
www.freespirit.com.

Library of Congress Cataloging-in-Publication Data
Names: Cummings, Rhoda Woods, author. | Fisher, Gary L. related work. Survival guide for kids
    with LD*,
Title: The survival guide for kids with LD* : (*learning differences) / Rhoda Cummings, Ed.D.
Description: Revised and updated third edition. | Golden Valley, MN : Free Spirit Publishing, 2016.
    | Revised edition of: The survival guide for kids with LD* : *learning differences / by Gary
    Fisher and Rhoda Cummings.
Identifiers: LCCN 2015044076 (print) | LCCN 2016004504 (ebook) | ISBN 9781631980312
    (paperback) | ISBN 1631980319 (soft cover) | ISBN 9781631980794 (Web pdf) | ISBN
    9781631980800 (epub)
Subjects: LCSH: Learning disabled children—Education—United States—Handbooks, manuals,
    etc.—Juvenile literature. | Learning disabilities—United States—Handbooks, manuals,
    etc.—Juvenile literature. | BISAC: JUVENILE NONFICTION / Social Issues / Special Needs.
    | JUVENILE NONFICTION / Social Issues / Self-Esteem & Self-Reliance. | JUVENILE
    NONFICTION / Social Issues / Emotions & Feelings.
Classification: LCC LC4705 .F57 2016 (print) | LCC LC4705 (ebook) | DDC 371.92—dc23
LC record available at http://lccn.loc.gov/2015044076

Free Spirit Publishing does not have control over or assume responsibility for author or third-
party websites and their content. At the time of this book's publication, all facts and figures
cited within are the most current available. All telephone numbers, addresses, and website URLs
are accurate and active; all publications, organizations, websites, and other resources exist as
described in this book; and all have been verified as of October 2015. If you find an error or believe
that a resource listed here is not as described, please contact Free Spirit Publishing. Parents,
teachers, and other adults: We strongly urge you to monitor children's use of the Internet.

Reading Level Grade 5; Interest Level Ages 9–14;
Fountas & Pinnell Guided Reading Level V

Edited by Kimberly Feltes Taylor
Cover and interior design by Emily Dyer
Illustrations by Ann Kronheimer

Additional graphics © Josemarques75 | Dreamstime.com; © Anastasiia Mishchenko | Dreamstime.com;
© Aliona Zbughin | Dreamstime.com; © Macrovector | Dreamstime.com; © Littlecuckoo | Dreamstime.com

10 9 8 7 6 5 4 3 2 1
Printed in the United States of America
B10950316

Free Spirit Publishing Inc.
6325 Sandburg Road, Suite 100
Golden Valley, MN 55427-3674
(612) 338-2068
help4kids@freespirit.com
www.freespirit.com

Free Spirit offers competitive pricing.
Contact edsales@freespirit.com for pricing information
on multiple quantity purchases.

Dedication

To Carter Cummings and Courtney Lantto,
the two best kids ever, and to Lloyd and
Madge Woods, the two best parents ever

Acknowledgments

First of all, a big thanks to Marjorie Lisovskis, the editorial director at Free Spirit Publishing, for suggesting this revision in the first place and for having confidence in me to take on this project. It has been so much fun to get back into the world of kids with LD. And thanks to my editor, Kimberly Feltes Taylor, who has masterfully and with great sensitivity taken my overabundance of words and turned them into a lively, upbeat book. And a very special thanks to Judy Galbraith, Free Spirit's publisher, who in the early days of Free Spirit shepherded along Gary Fisher and me while we wrote the first *Survival Guide*. Neither Gary nor I could ever have imagined its success over the years.

Thank you, Gary Fisher, for having me as your coauthor for the first *Survival Guide*. I have loved working with you over the years. I hope you are pleased with this revision.

And finally, thanks to my son Carter for his tenacity, resilience, and independent spirit as he's traveled along a sometimes bumpy road. And to every other kid and adult with LD: Stay strong!

Contents

Introduction 1
   Welcome to This Book! 2
   How This Book Can Help You 2
   How to Use This Book 3
   Features in the Book 4
   Write to Me 5
   The Six Great Gripes of Kids with LD 6

Chapter 1 • What Is LD? 7
   What LD Means for Different Kids 8
   What LD Does Not Mean 10
   Why Do Some Kids Have LD? 11
   How Adults Find Out That a Kid Has LD 12
   Checklist—Find Out About Yourself 14

Chapter 2 • Seven Kinds of LD 16
   1. Problems with Reading 16
   2. Problems with Writing 17
   3. Problems with Math 19
   4. Problems with Understanding What You See 20
   5. Problems with Understanding What
      You Hear 22
   6. Problems with Understanding Language 23
   7. Problems with Nonverbal Skills 25
   LD and Other Problems 26
   Checklist—Find Out About Your LD 28

Chapter 3 • Why Is It Hard for Kids with LD to Learn? 30
Seeing and Hearing 30
How Information Gets to the Brain 31
Receiving the Signals—or Input 31
Making Sense of the Signals—or Integration 32
Using What You've Learned—or Output 33
Getting Help 34
Quiz—Your Brain and LD 35

Chapter 4 • Learning with Assistive Technology 38
What Is Assistive Technology? 38
Types of Assistive Technology 39
Quiz—Assistive Technology:
    Remembering What Helps What 44

Chapter 5 • Ten Ways to Get Along Better in School 46
1. When Things Are Tough, Have a Chat 47
2. Keep Your Head Up! 48
3. Become an Expert 49
4. Take Part in School Activities 49
5. Make Friends 50
6. Be a Helper 50
7. Stay Out of Trouble 51
8. Know How to Relax and Cool Off 52
9. Do Not Use LD as an Excuse! 52
10. Learn More About LD 53
Tips Just for Recess and the Playground 54
Tips Just for the Cafeteria 55
Reflective Questions—How Will You Get Along? . . 57

**Chapter 6 • How to Get Along Better in
School When You Get Older** .... .58
Tips Just for Middle School 58
Tips Just for High School 60
Checklist—What Will You Do to Get
    Along Better? 62

**Chapter 7 • Five Rules (and Tips!) for
Making and Keeping Friends** .... .63
Social Rule #1: Be Careful About What You Say.... 63
Social Rule #2: Wait for Your Turn to Talk 65
Social Rule #3: Pay Attention to
    Nonverbal Signals 66
Social Rule #4: Recognize a Mistake 68
Social Rule #5: Be a Good Friend 70
Quiz—Do You Know the Social Rules? 72

Chapter 8 • How to Deal with Bullying .... .74
Teasing versus Bullying 75
Four Types of Bullying 75
Reasons Why Kids Bully 77
How to Handle Bullying 77
Checklist—How Will You Handle Bullying? 80

**Chapter 9 • How to Deal with Sad, Hurt,
and Angry Feelings** .... .81
Why Kids with LD Have These Feelings 81
Six Ways to Help Yourself Feel Better 84
Reflective Questions—Dealing with
    Your Feelings 88

**Chapter 10 • Ten Tips for Getting Along
Better at Home** 89
   1. Tell Your Parents You Need Time to Relax 91
   2. Tell Your Parents If Your Homework
      Takes Too Long 92
   3. Help Your Parents Understand Your LD 93
   4. Tell Your Parents Good News About Yourself . . 94
   5. Take Time Out When You Need It 95
   6. Make a Plan for Your Schoolwork 95
   7. Eat Well 96
   8. Get a Pet 96
   9. Find a Hobby 97
  10. Get a Job 97
   Checklist—What Will You Do? 98

Chapter 11 • What About the Future? 99
   School After High School 100
   On the Job 103
   Reflective Questions—Your Life After
      High School 106

**Chapter 12 • IDEA: A Law to Help Kids
with LD Learn** 107
   Important Parts of IDEA 108
   What the Law Means for Students with LD 109
   Reflective Questions—How Do You
      Learn Best? 113

Chapter 13 • Getting into an LD Program . . .114
   Other Kinds of Kids with Special Needs 114
   How LD Is First Noticed 115
   How Did You Get into an LD Program? 117
   Quiz—Getting Help for LD 120

Chapter 14 • A Happy Ending: You Can Be a Winner! 122

Resources for You 124

A Note to Parents and Teachers 127

Index 130

About the Author 135

Introduction

- Do you have trouble with schoolwork even though you think you are smart?

- Do you try to listen to your teacher but you cannot tune out other noises and movement in the room?

- Do you have a hard time following directions at school?

- Do you have difficulty remembering your assignments and other things?

- Do you get in trouble at school sometimes and you don't know why?

- Do you wish you had more friends, but you just do not know how to say and do the right things?

- Do you feel different—like you do not know where you fit in?

- Do you feel all alone in the world, as if no one really understands you—including yourself?

If you can say YES to any of these questions, then keep reading!

Welcome to This Book!

Hello! My name is Rhoda Cummings. If you have LD, this book can help you. LD stands for "learning difference" or "learning disability" (read more about this in Chapter 1). I wrote this book because I understand how hard it can be to have LD. My son Carter has LD. Even though school was hard for him at times, he is grown up now and doing well. He has worked at the same job for nearly 20 years, has good friends, and is happy with his life.

I also am a teacher. For over 30 years, I have taught kids with LD, and I have taught college students studying to be teachers of students with LD. I wrote this book for you to use as a guide when you need help with school, at home, and with your friends.

How This Book Can Help You

This book will not clear up all your problems. But it can help you understand yourself better. It can give you some ideas about how to make school better for yourself. It can help you get ready for the future.

Over the years, I have found that kids with LD ask the same questions about LD. They often ask:

- Why do kids with LD have trouble learning?
- What can kids with LD do about having LD?
- Are kids with LD stupid?
- Why do kids with LD have a hard time in school?
- Why don't other kids understand kids with LD?

This book will answer those questions and many more you may have.

How to Use This Book

You can use this book however you want. You can read it from beginning to end. Or you can page through it for parts that interest you. (Check out the Contents. It might help you decide how to read the book.) You can read the book once. Or you can read it many times. You can read it before you go to bed at night. Or you can read it when you first wake up or throughout the day. The most important thing is to use it in a way that works for you.

You can read this book on your own or you can ask your parents* to read it with you. If you read the book on your own, talk to a parent or another trusted grown-up as you read the book. Talk about what you learn from the book. If you see an idea in the book that you think will help you, talk about how you can use that idea.

*When you see "parents" in this book, think of the person or people who are raising you. That may be your mom or dad. That may be a grandparent or an aunt, uncle, or older sibling. Or that may be another adult.

If you are in a class with other students who have LD, show the book to your teacher. Your teacher may want to read the book with the whole class.

Features in the Book

This book includes stories and quotations from real kids with LD just like you. They talk about their challenges in school, with friends, and at home. They also talk about their successes and their fears and hopes for the future.

Sophia* is in eighth grade. She has LD. She has a hard time with reading. But she is an expert horse rider. She wins ribbons when she rides in horseshows.

At the end of each chapter, you'll find an activity. The activity may have you check items in a list that apply to you. The activity may be a quick, fun quiz. Or the activity may be a set of questions to think about again and again. You can photocopy the page from the book or download and print out a copy of these activities at www.freespirit.com/LD. Then fill them out. The activities will help you find out more about yourself and your LD. After doing an activity, you may want to share your

*This book does not use people's real names. The names are made up to respect people's privacy.

thoughts with a parent, teacher, other trusted grown-up, sibling, or friend. Sharing your thoughts will help other people understand you and how LD affects you.

Write to Me

After you finish reading *The Survival Guide for Kids with LD*, you may want to write to me. I would be glad to hear from you! Tell me how the book helped you. Tell me about your challenges and successes. Give me ideas for making the book even better. If you are a parent or teacher and have questions about LD, write to me, too!

You can send a letter to:
Rhoda Cummings
c/o Free Spirit Publishing
6325 Sandburg Road, Suite 100
Golden Valley, MN 55427-3674

Or you can email me at:
help4kids@freespirit.com

Best wishes,
Rhoda Cummings

The Six Great Gripes of Kids with LD

Here are the six things that kids with LD say bother them the most:

1. No one tells me what LD is, so I spend a lot of time worrying about what is wrong with me.

2. I feel confused in school about what I am supposed to do.

3. My parents, teachers, and the other kids are often not patient with me.

4. I do not have many friends.

5. I get in trouble and I don't know why.

6. I do not like being called retarded, stupid, or dumb.

What Is LD?

When someone has LD, it means that the person "learns differently." People with LD learn differently because their brains handle—or process—information differently. Sometimes, people think of LD as a "learning disability." But having LD doesn't mean you aren't able to learn—it just means you learn in your own way. You may even learn some things better than kids who don't have LD. So when you see the term "LD" in this book, think of it as meaning "learns differently."

Drake

Drake has LD. He is 12 years old. He reads out loud to understand the words better.

What LD Means for Different Kids

Not all kids with LD are the same. Some have only a few problems learning. They may be great in reading, but they have problems learning in another area, such as math. Others have problems learning everything from writing to math, reading, and spelling. They might even have trouble learning how to make friends.

A few students have a tough time with all of their schoolwork. But they may quickly learn other things like playing the piano, building a model airplane, or using the latest technology.

Juan

Juan is in seventh grade. He has LD. He has trouble reading. But he is a whiz with technology. He even helps other kids when they don't know how to work their tablets or apps.

Elisa

Elisa also has LD. She is 10 years old. She has a hard time with reading and math. But she is an amazing artist. An art gallery in her town shows her paintings.

Thinking about sports may help you better understand LD. For example, not all players on a football team can throw a ball like the quarterback. Instead, they can block players on the other team, they can run really fast, or they can kick the football through the goal post. All players on the team can play football, but they each play differently from each other. Similarly, all kids with LD can learn, they just learn differently from other kids.

What LD Does Not Mean

Saying exactly what LD means can be difficult. But everyone agrees on what LD does *not* mean:

- It does not mean you are dumb.*
- It does not mean you are lazy.
- It does not mean you cannot learn.
- It does not mean you cannot go to college.
- It does not mean you will have a low-paying job when you grow up.
- It does not mean you cannot have a good life as an adult.

*Many kids with LD have higher than average intelligence.

You might wish you did not have LD, but do not let LD stop you from becoming the best person you can be. Sometimes, you will have to work harder than other kids. You will also need to work with your parents and teachers to come up with plans for learning that are best for you. But you *can* meet the challenge of LD.

Why Do Some Kids Have LD?

We know that the brain processes information differently in kids with LD. But we do not always know why some kids have LD when others do not. And we do not know why there are so many different ways to have LD. Furthermore, nobody knows exactly what causes someone's brain to process information differently. However, scientists have several ideas about the causes of LD.

Some kids with LD had problems before—or while—they were born. Maybe their mother was sick or was injured. Or maybe they had a hard time being born. During a long and difficult delivery, a baby might have a hard time breathing. The baby's brain might not get enough oxygen. Not getting enough oxygen can cause LD. Being born too early can also cause LD.

Some kids with LD had problems right after being born. Maybe they got very sick right after being born. A head injury early in life can also cause LD.

Some kids with LD inherited LD. If kids have aunts, uncles, or parents with LD, the kids could have LD, too. But there are many people who seem to be the only ones in their families with LD.

However, until we learn more about LD, this is the best thing we can say about it: Some kids need to learn in a different way. And nobody knows exactly why. But knowing the cause of LD is not as important as getting the help you need.

How Adults Find Out That a Kid Has LD

Some kids have problems learning from a very early age. Parents may notice that their kids have a hard time learning to catch a ball, staying in the lines when they color, or understanding the rules of a game. Maybe they have trouble learning to talk, or they cannot understand what other people are saying.

However, most kids with LD don't seem to have trouble learning until they start school. They may have trouble understanding directions the teacher gives or keeping up with the classwork. They may have trouble learning to read. They might not understand about numbers. They start falling behind their classmates.

After two or three years, they have fallen far enough behind that the school tests them (if their parents say it is okay) to see if they have LD. The tests can help tell if they have LD. If they do, they may spend part of the day getting extra help from a specialist in a resource room.

Rebecca is 10 years old. She can read the words in her book. But she has trouble understanding what the words mean. The LD specialist shows Rebecca ways to understand better.

Rebecca

Some kids with LD may catch up with their class-mates. Then they will no longer work with a specialist. But most kids with LD will continue to work with a specialist until they graduate from school.

If you have been told that you have LD, you are lucky. Someone who cared for you—your mother, father, or a teacher—noticed that you learned differently and took steps to get help for you.

Find Out About Yourself

Chapter 1 helped you understand LD better. Answer the questions below to understand yourself better. (Pssst! There are no right or wrong answers.) Write your answers in a notebook. Or photocopy the checklist to write on. Or you can download and print out a copy at www.freespirit.com/LD.

Check the item that best describes you for each question.

1. How has having LD made you think about yourself?

☐ Sometimes I think I'm dumb and can't learn.

☐ I can learn—I just learn differently from other kids.

2. What do you think caused your LD?

☐ I had problems before or while being born.

☐ I had an illness or injury just after being born.

☐ I have a relative with LD.

☐ I don't know the cause.

From *The Survival Guide for Kids with LD* by Rhoda Cummings, Ed.D., copyright © 2016. This page may be reproduced for individual, classroom, or small group use only. For other uses, contact Free Spirit Publishing Inc. at freespirit.com/permissions.

3. When did you first know that you had LD?

☐ I knew before I started school.
☐ I knew after I started school.
☐ I am just finding out now.

4. Who was the first person to help you find out why you had trouble learning?

☐ A parent helped me.
☐ A teacher helped me.
☐ Another adult helped me.

5. What is your plan for making learning easier? (Check all that apply.)

☐ I will ask my parents for help.
☐ I will ask my teachers for help.
☐ I will keep reading this book.

Do you know yourself a little bit better now? As you continue to read the book, keep your understanding of yourself in mind. Think about how the information you read can help you.

From *The Survival Guide for Kids with LD* by Rhoda Cummings, Ed.D., copyright © 2016. This page may be reproduced for individual, classroom, or small group use only. For other uses, contact Free Spirit Publishing Inc. at freespirit.com/permissions.

Chapter 2

Seven Kinds of LD

You learned in Chapter 1 that some kids may only have trouble with reading *or* math. Other kids may have trouble with reading *and* math. Their LD may even cause problems in other areas, too.

LD can affect different kids in different ways. Reading about the different kinds of LD—and the problems related to LD—will help you better understand it. Here are seven kinds of LD someone might have.

1. Problems with Reading

One kind of LD causes kids to have many problems with reading. They may have trouble recognizing words they know. They have trouble with spelling and may see the letters in the wrong order. They may read much slower than other kids. They might have trouble learning the alphabet or sounding out words. They might also read some lines more than once. They might have a hard time understanding what they read. They might also write letters or words backward. This kind of LD is called *dyslexia*.

Aleisha says it was hard for her to read. She read letters backward. Sometimes, she read words backward. She works with an LD teacher several times a week to learn ways to read letters and words the right way. Now reading is easier for her.

Aleisha

Do you have problems with reading? These two tips might help you.

Use a ruler. Place the ruler under the words you are reading. It will help you focus on the words in the sentence that you are supposed to be reading.

Read out loud when you can. If you use your ears as well as your eyes when you read, you will be more likely to remember what you have read.

2. Problems with Writing

Some kids have a type of LD that makes writing hard. They have many ideas in their heads and can talk about them, but they have trouble putting them down on paper. They may leave out letters or whole words. They may add extra space between letters or words. They may have a hard time holding the pen or pencil. Their handwriting might be hard to read. They may move their paper around as they write. Their school papers might be very messy. This kind of LD is called *dysgraphia*.

Jermaine takes a long time to put his thoughts on paper, and his writing is hard to read. He is very excited because he learned to write using a computer. He used to get low grades for messy papers. His papers had holes in them from erasing mistakes over and over. Now he can fix his mistakes on the computer, and he can turn in neat, clean papers.

Do you have problems with writing? These two tips might help you with writing.

Practice writing movements. Spend 10 or 15 minutes each day using a pencil to draw shapes, such as the shape of a letter. Write each letter from A to Z five times. Write each number from 1 to 10 five times. But any shape will do. Make circles or squares. For more shape ideas, go to YouTube.com. Type in "Zen Doodles." The video will show you many fun shapes to draw.

Hold your pencil or pen the correct way. Hold your pencil or pen between your thumb and middle finger. Place your index finger (your pointer finger) on top of the pencil or pen. Your thumb and index finger should be just above the point. Let the pencil rest on your middle finger. Holding your pencil correctly will give you better control. Your writing may get neater.

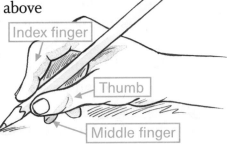

Index finger

Thumb

Middle finger

Do you have trouble remembering where to hold the pencil or pen? Put a rubber band around the place where you should hold it.

Is the pencil or pen too skinny to hold easily? Get a "finger grip." A grip slides over the pencil or pen and makes it easier to hold. Stores like Target, Walmart, and Amazon.com sell them.

3. Problems with Math

Another kind of LD causes kids to have trouble with numbers. Addition and subtraction problems are difficult for them. They may not understand what the numbers or symbols mean in math problems. They might have trouble lining up numbers when writing down math problems and answers. They may also have trouble memorizing multiplication tables or the steps for solving a math problem. Even if they memorize how to do something in math, they may not understand what the answer means. This kind of LD is called *dyscalculia*.

Kids with dyscalculia sometimes have trouble with directions like left and right. They also may have problems with measurement, how to tell time, or how to count money.

Shayla

Shayla has trouble remembering the steps for adding and subtracting. She gets special help in math. Her teacher lets her use a calculator to add and subtract. That way she can continue to learn about fractions and the number line.

Do you have problems with math? These two tips might help you.

Memorize the facts. Write down the facts. Use flash cards. Write addition, subtraction, multiplication, and division problems on them. Write the problems on one side. Write the answers on the other side. Play games with them. Practice with a friend. Try to memorize a new math fact every day.

Use your fingers. Count, add, and subtract by raising or dropping a finger.

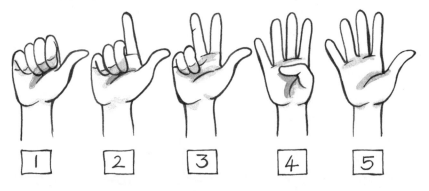

4. Problems with Understanding What You See

Another kind of LD makes it difficult for kids to *understand* what they see. They can see just fine. There is nothing wrong with their eyes. But their brains have trouble understanding what they are seeing. Kids with this kind of LD may have trouble remembering what a photograph or chart shows because they can't keep an image of it in their heads. They may have trouble with reading because they cannot focus on the words on a page. They may skip lines when they read or only see the white background of the paper. This kind of LD is called *visual perceptual/visual motor deficit*.

Logan

Logan says that when he tries to read, the black printed words move around on the white page. So Logan uses audiobooks and other recordings of texts and teacher instructions. That way, he can learn and know what to do from listening, not reading.

Do you have problems with understanding what you see? These two tips might help you.

Ask for recorded instructions. Talk to your parents about meeting with your teacher. At the meeting, ask if your teacher will record assignment instructions on your cell phone, tablet, or computer. That way, you will not have to read the instructions for the assignment. You can listen to them.

Ask for fewer items on a page. At the meeting with your teacher, ask if he or she can put just four problems or questions on a handout. So if the assignment has 20 problems, you would get five pages, each with four problems. You'll be able to focus on each problem more easily than if they were all on the same page.

5. Problems with Understanding What You Hear

Some kids have a type of LD that causes them not to *understand* what they hear. Kids with this kind of LD can hear just fine. But their brains have trouble understanding what they are hearing. So when someone says the word "fight," their brains might interpret—or hear—the word as "fit." Or their brains might think someone is saying "old" instead of "cold." This kind of LD is called *auditory processing disorder*.

Kids with this kind of LD may have trouble following the instructions a teacher tells the class. They can also get confused when there is too much noise in the classroom. They may hear everything at the same time and not be able to focus on what the teacher is saying.

Emma

Emma is in eighth grade. In science class, the kids sometimes work in groups. When kids in other groups are talking, Emma has a hard time focusing on what the kids in her own group are saying. So Emma asks her group members to lean toward her when they talk. That way, she can better focus on what they are saying. They are happy to make sure she understands them.

Do you have problems with understanding what you hear? These two tips might help you.

Sit in the front. If you sit close to your teacher, you can focus on what she is saying. You won't hear the other kids as much.

Ask for written instructions. Talk to your parents about meeting with your teacher. At the meeting, they can ask your teacher to write down your assignment instructions. You may understand the instructions better if you read them than if you hear them.

6. Problems with Understanding Language

This kind of LD is a type of auditory processing disorder (the LD explained in number 5). But it relates just to language. So kids with this type of LD may be able to tune out background noises. But they have trouble understanding what people are saying. They also often feel that they can't find the right words to explain their own ideas and thoughts to others. They also may have problems with reading and writing. This type of LD is called *language processing disorder.*

Shawn

Shawn's teacher told his class about the different kinds of points on an arrow. She asked for a volunteer to repeat the different kinds of points. Shawn raised his hand. He said, "The first kind is the decimal point." All the kids laughed at him. Shawn felt bad. He didn't know what was funny. His teacher had asked about points. So he answered with the only point he could think of—the decimal point that is used with numbers. Because he has auditory processing disorder, Shawn didn't remember that the teacher had been talking about arrow points. The LD specialist worked with Shawn. She taught him how to think about the answer to a question before he says it aloud.

Do you have problems with understanding language? These two tips might help you. (Check out the tips for Problems with Understanding What You Hear, number 5. They might help you, too.)

Speak up. If you don't understand what your teacher or someone else says, ask them to repeat themselves. You could say, "Could you please repeat that?" Or you could say, "I'm sorry. I didn't understand you. Could you say that again?"

Practice your answers. Write down words to explain your ideas. Then practice reading your ideas out loud. Ask a parent or your teacher to listen to your ideas and help you tell what you really want to say.

7. Problems with Nonverbal Skills

Sometimes kids with LD read, write, and do math well. But they have trouble "reading" people. They laugh or speak at the wrong time and interrupt conversations. They do not get jokes that their friends tell. They stand too close to the person they are talking to. This kind of LD is called *nonverbal learning disabilities*.

Aoki

Aoki has a hard time making friends. He often interrupts when other people are talking. His classmates sometimes call him pushy. Aoki works with an LD teacher who is helping him "read" other people's body signals. Now he does not interrupt as much. He gets along a lot better with his classmates.

Kids with this kind of LD may also have a hard time controlling their muscles. They might have trouble running, riding a bike, jumping, hopping, and playing sports. They lose their balance easily. They are teased for being clumsy. Some kids have trouble holding a pencil or using scissors. Their handwriting is hard to read. They also have trouble buttoning their shirt, tying their shoes, or using forks and spoons during meals.

Do you have problems with nonverbal skills? These two tips might help you.

Study nonverbal signals. Ask a family member or friend to make faces to show that they are mad, sad, worried, or excited. Say the feeling that you think goes with the facial expression. Practice until you are able to "read" the facial expressions. Do the same thing for body language signals.

Practice moving through space. Make a curved path out of chairs or stools. Practice walking around the objects. Pay attention to how close you are to them—or how far away. This will help you know how close you are to objects and people.

LD and Other Problems

Often, kids with LD also have *attention deficit hyperactivity disorder* (ADHD). Some of these kids have a difficult time paying attention to one thing. Too much noise or too many pictures can make it hard for them to focus on what someone is saying or trying to show them. Some kids with ADHD may not have attention problems. But they move around all the time. They simply can't sit still. Other kids with ADHD have problems both with paying attention and with sitting still.

Kids with LD may also have problems with *executive functioning.* They have a hard time remembering things. They may have trouble remembering information for a test or how to solve a math problem. These kids may also have problems with organization. They leave their homework at home or in their locker. They go to class with the wrong book or they lose their book. Their desks and rooms at home look like they were hit by a tornado. They may also have a hard time keeping track of time. So they are often late.

Kids with LD who work with a specialist can get help for these other problems. The specialist will help them learn how to focus on one thing and sit still. The specialist will give them tips for remembering things, staying organized, and being on time.

We were supposed to meet at 3:00.

Paul

Paul is in college. He has LD and ADHD. In high school, Paul went to the resource specialist for help until he graduated. He learned ways to focus his attention. He still has ADHD. But now he knows how to focus. He gets good grades in college.

Find Out About Your LD

What kind of LD do you have? Some kids have more than one kind. Write down the kinds that you have on a separate sheet of paper. Or make a photocopy of the checklist to mark your answers. Or you can download and print out a copy at www.freespirit.com/LD.

Check all the kinds of LD that apply to you.

☐ I have problems with reading.
(dyslexia)

☐ I have problems with writing.
(dysgraphia)

☐ I have problems with math.
(dyscalculia)

☐ I have problems understanding what I see.
(visual perceptual/visual motor deficit)

☐ I have problems understanding what I hear.
(auditory processing disorder)

☐ I have problems with language.
(language processing disorder)

☐ I have problems with nonverbal skills.
(nonverbal learning disabilities)

→

From *The Survival Guide for Kids with LD* by Rhoda Cummings, Ed.D., copyright © 2016. This page may be reproduced for individual, classroom, or small group use only. For other uses, contact Free Spirit Publishing Inc. at freespirit.com/permissions.

Do you have problems related to LD?

☐ I have problems paying attention.
(attention deficit hyperactivity disorder)

☐ I have problems sitting still.
(attention deficit hyperactivity disorder)

☐ I have problems remembering things.
(executive functioning)

☐ I have problems keeping things organized.
(executive functioning)

☐ I have problems being on time.
(executive functioning)

Keep reading the book. As you read, think about the kind of LD you have. Think about how the information in the book can help you with your LD.

From *The Survival Guide for Kids with LD* by Rhoda Cummings, Ed.D., copyright © 2016. This page may be reproduced for individual, classroom, or small group use only. For other uses, contact Free Spirit Publishing Inc. at freespirit.com/permissions.

Chapter 3

Why Is It Hard for Kids with LD to Learn?

In Chapter 2, you learned about the different kinds of LD. Maybe you gained a better understanding of your own LD. In Chapter 3, you'll learn why having LD makes it difficult for you to learn.

Seeing and Hearing

Kids with LD sometimes feel like they see and hear things differently. Do you feel like you see and hear things differently? To find out, ask yourself these questions:

- Do I have trouble when I try to spell a word?
- When I try to read, do I skip over words or lines?
- When someone tells a joke, do I laugh at the wrong time?
- When my teacher gives directions, can I only remember part of them?
- Do I often feel like I don't understand what I am reading, seeing, or hearing?

Though some kids with LD may have a vision or hearing problem, the truth is: most kids with LD see and hear just fine. For kids with LD, the problems with "hearing" and "seeing" take place in the brain—not in the eyes and ears.

How Information Gets to the Brain

As you look around and see things, your eyes turn what they see into signals. Then your eyes send the signals to your brain. Your brain then "tells" you what you are seeing. Your ears work the same way. They turn the sounds they hear into signals. Then they send the signals to your brain. The brain "tells" you what you are hearing.

Receiving the Signals—or Input

In kids with LD, the brain has trouble receiving the signals. The brain may flip the signals. Let's say you are looking at the letter "b." Your eyes send the signal for "b" to your brain. But your brain receives the signal as "d." Your brain has flipped the signal. Your brain may also have trouble knowing which signals are the important ones. So when you read, you may skip a word. The same problems can occur with numbers and math.

The brain can also have the same problems receiving signals related to hearing. So you may hear the word "stop." But your brain receives it as "top." Your brain might also have trouble tuning out unimportant sounds. So you have trouble focusing on the important sounds, such as your teacher speaking.

Ethan

Ethan has LD. When he tries to listen to his teacher, his brain gives all the other sounds in the classroom the same importance—so he hears them "all at once." An LD specialist helps Ethan learn how to block out sounds that are not important.

Making Sense of the Signals— or Integration

After receiving the signals, your brain has to organize the signals. It also has to understand the meaning behind the signals. In kids with LD, the brain might have trouble with organizing and understanding the signals.

Let's say you are reading. You get to the word "top." Your eyes send signals to your brain for "t" – "o" – "p." Your brain receives the signals. It doesn't flip them or skip them. However, your brain organizes them in the wrong way. So instead of organizing the signals as "top," your brain organizes the signals as "opt" or "tpo." Or, your brain may organize the signals as "top," but it can't make sense of what "top" means. You may actually know what "top" means. If asked, you may be able to explain what a "top" is. You may be able to give an example of a "top." But in that moment of reading, your brain just can't make sense of the word.

The same thing can happen with signals related to numbers for math problems. It can also happen with sounds.

Using What You've Learned— or Output

Kids with LD often have trouble expressing themselves. They may have problems answering a question in a conversation. They may have difficulty writing down their ideas. Sometimes, they know they *know* the information. But their brain can't find the information at that moment. Their brain is having problems sending out signals. It can't *output* the information. Other times, they have the idea in their head that they want to express. But they can't get the words out when speaking. Or they can't put the words or numbers on paper. Their brain is also having problems sending out signals.

Getting Help

With all of these different signal mix ups, no wonder it's hard to learn! But even if your brain works differently, you *can* learn. LD specialists have ways to help. If you have problems with what you "see" and "hear," talk to your parents. Talk to them about getting help. Talk to your teachers, too. Talk about ways you can learn differently. For example, if you read well, but have a hard time hearing things your teacher says, then maybe your teacher can write down your assignment instructions. Here are some other ways to learn differently:

- At home, read aloud instead of silently. At school, ask your teacher where you can read aloud without bothering other students.

- Put a ruler or a strip of cardboard under the line of text you are reading to help you follow the text and keep your place as you read.

- Build a model or draw a picture instead of writing a report (but first, ask your teacher if this is okay).

- Write math problems on graph paper to line up the numbers straight.

- Ask your teacher if you can have extra time when taking tests.

The most important thing to remember is: If you need help, ask! Do not keep your problems with learning a secret.

Check out this site for more information about the brain: **faculty.washington.edu/chudler/split.html**

Your Brain and LD

Quiz

How does LD make learning difficult for you? Answer the following questions to find out. You can write your answers (just the letters) on a separate sheet of paper. Or you can photocopy the quiz to write on. Or you can download and print out a copy at www.freespirit.com/LD. Look at the second and third pages to find out what your answers mean.

1. **How does your brain work when your teacher asks you a question?**
   a. I can hear the question, but I can't find the answer in my brain.
   b. I can find the answer in my brain, but it doesn't come out of my mouth the right way.
   c. I can't answer the question if it is too long.
   d. I can't answer the question if I have to write it down. But if I can say the answer, I can do it.

2. **How does your brain work when you read a book?**
   a. I sometimes read the words wrong.
   b. I sometimes leave out important words.
   c. I can read words, but I don't understand what some of the words mean.
   d. The words get all jumbled together.

From *The Survival Guide for Kids with LD* by Rhoda Cummings, Ed.D., copyright © 2016. This page may be reproduced for individual, classroom, or small group use only. For other uses, contact Free Spirit Publishing Inc. at freespirit.com/permissions.

3. **How does your brain work when you try to write down a word in a spelling test?**

   a. I can hear the word but I write it down backward.
   b. I write down the wrong word.
   c. I hear the word but when I write it down, I jumble the letters.
   d. I can hear the word and see how it is spelled in my brain. But when I try to write it, I spell it the wrong way.

What Your Answers Mean

Question 1:

- If you answered **a**: You have trouble organizing the information. Your brain cannot make sense of the question.

- If you answered **b**: You understand the question and your brain has organized the information, but you have trouble getting the information out of your brain.

- If you answered **c**: You have trouble receiving too much information at the same time. Your brain wants to take in all of the information. It is not able to pay attention to the most important information.

- If you answered **d**: You understand the question and you know the answer. It's just that your brain does not know how to answer in writing. But your brain can answer the question when you use your speech.

From *The Survival Guide for Kids with LD* by Rhoda Cummings, Ed.D., copyright © 2016. This page may be reproduced for individual, classroom, or small group use only. For other uses, contact Free Spirit Publishing Inc. at freespirit.com/permissions.

Question 2:

- If you answered **a**: Your eyes see the word but your brain organizes the word signal wrong. Your brain cannot make sense of the signal.

- If you answered **b**: Your brain has trouble knowing which signals are important. It does not recognize the right signal for the word.

- If you answered **c**: Your brain has received the word signal from your eyes. But it organizes the word in the wrong way. It can't make sense of the word.

- If you answered **d**: Your eyes see the words. Your brain receives the information. But when you try to understand the words, the brain can't send out the signal that tells what the words mean.

Question 3:

- If you answered **a**: Your brain flips the signal for the word.

- If you answered **b**: Your brain receives the wrong signal for the word.

- If you answered **c**: Your brain receives the right signal for the word, but your brain organizes the signal for the word in the wrong way.

- If you answered **d**: You know how to spell the word but your brain cannot *output* the word. You cannot put the word down on paper.

As you continue to read the book, think about how your brain works. Think about what advice is most helpful for how your brain works.

From *The Survival Guide for Kids with LD* by Rhoda Cummings, Ed.D., copyright © 2016. This page may be reproduced for individual, classroom, or small group use only. For other uses, contact Free Spirit Publishing Inc. at freespirit.com/permissions.

Learning with Assistive Technology

Chapter 3 helped you understand why kids with LD have difficulty learning. It gave you a better understanding of LD in general as well as your own LD. The next step is to start getting the help you need. Chapter 4 will tell you about a great way to get help with learning—through assistive technology.

> **assistive technology
> (ah SIS tiv TEK nahl o gee)**
>
> Technology that helps with learning.

What Is Assistive Technology?

Assistive technology is pretty much what it sounds like—technology that assists, or helps, with learning. Assistive technology helps kids with LD learn by giving them a different *way* to learn. For example, if you have trouble with reading, you can use a type of assistive technology that will read the text aloud to you—so you can learn the information in the text by hearing it.

Assistive technology does not fix the learning difficulty. But it helps you work around the learning difficulty—so that you can learn what everyone else is learning.

Types of Assistive Technology

Just as they are many different types of LD, there are many different types of assistive technology.

Audiobooks. Listening to an audiobook—or a recording of text—can be helpful for kids with LD who have trouble with reading but can understand what they hear. Recordings exist for a wide variety of books, magazine articles, and other types of texts. Recordings can be downloaded to your computer, tablet, or phone. Some audiobook apps include features that allow you to search the recording. They also allow you to mark places in the recording that you might want to go back to later.

Optical character recognition systems. Not all text has a recorded version. For example, it's unlikely that the directions at the top of a worksheet have a recorded version. But you can use a special tool to scan the text. The tool recognizes the text and reads it aloud—so you can hear the text. Some scanners are pocket-sized. You can carry the scanner with you, wherever you go.

Alternative keyboards. Some kids with LD have trouble using the standard keyboard for a computer. They may have a hard time controlling their fingers and hitting the small keys correctly. Or they may have difficulty understanding how the keyboard is organized. There are different types of alternative keyboards that can help with these problems. Some alternative keyboards have larger keys, so they are easier to hit. Some alternative keyboards organize the keys in a different way that makes more sense to someone with LD. They may also have color-coded keys. Or they may use different symbols.

Speech recognition programs. With this tool, you "write" by "speaking." The speech recognition program recognizes what you are saying and displays the words on your screen. These programs exist for computers, tablets, and phones. So you can "speak" your book reports and other schoolwork. You can also "speak" your notes and reminders to yourself, rather than writing them down. This tool is useful for kids with LD who know what they want to write but have difficulty when trying to write the words.

Lily

Lily has lots of good ideas in her head, but she has trouble when she tries to write them down for class assignments. Now, she has a speech recognition program on her laptop. She says her ideas out loud and they show up on the screen. Her grades are much better!

Recorders. A recorder is another useful tool for kids with LD who have difficulty with writing. Rather than writing down the instructions your teacher gives you, you can record your teacher saying the instructions. Kids with LD who have difficulty with reading also find recordings to be useful. They can listen to the instructions later, rather than trying to read what they had written down. Recordings are also helpful for kids with LD who have trouble with understanding what they hear. They can replay the recording over and over—and even slow it down—until they understand what is being said.

Personal FM listening systems. Kids with LD who are distracted by background noises and have difficulty focusing on what their teacher says may benefit from using this device. The teacher has a small microphone. The student has a small receiver. Some receivers are small enough to fit around your ear. Other students

might not even notice it. The system is wireless, so there is no cable connecting the microphone to the receiver. The microphone picks up the teacher's words. The words are sent to the receiver. So the words go right into your ears and are easier to focus on.

Electronic math worksheets. These worksheets are helpful for kids with LD who have trouble lining up problems correctly when working with pencil and paper. You complete the worksheet on a computer or tablet. You use the keyboard to enter numbers for the problem. The electronic worksheet keeps the numbers correctly lined up as you work through addition, subtraction, multiplication, or division problems. Some electronic worksheets have speech recognition. They understand what you say aloud. So you can talk through the problem, rather than entering numbers with the keyboard. Some electronic worksheets can also read aloud the problem and your answer.

Talking calculators. These calculators say the number as you press the key for a number. They also say the operation as you press the key for that operation, such as "divide." Talking calculators are useful for kids with LD who have a hard time "reading" numbers. You hear what you are entering, so you can make sure that you are pressing the correct buttons in the correct order. These calculators also say the answer that is calculated.

If you think assistive technology would help you, talk to your parents. Your parents might want to talk to your teachers and the LD specialist. Together, you can figure out which assistive technology will best help you. Not every type of assistive technology can help with your LD. So you need to find the right one for you.

The list on pages 39–42 tells about the most commonly used types of assistive technology. But there are many other tools that can help you read, write, listen, do math, and organize your thoughts in other ways, too. So if none of the devices and programs you read about here seem right for you, ask if there is something else that would help you.

Another good reason to have your parents talk to your teachers and the LD specialist is that your school might have equipment that you can use. That way, your parents won't have to spend money on new equipment.

AssistiveTechnology: Remembering What Helps What

Assistive technology can be very helpful. Do you remember how? Find out by answering the following questions. (Don't worry! This quiz is just for fun.) Write your answers (just the letters) on a separate sheet of paper. Or photocopy the quiz to write on. Or you can download and print out a copy of the quiz at www.freespirit.com/LD. Check your answers at the end of the quiz.

1. **Brent always has great ideas for his book reports and research papers. He knows what he wants to write. But he has a hard time getting his words down on paper. Which type of assistive technology might help him?**

   a. audiobooks
   b. speech recognition programs
   c. personal FM listening systems

2. **Ana has a hard time remembering what her teachers say. So when she gets home, she isn't sure what to do for homework. Which type of assistive technology might help her?**

   a. optical character recognition systems
   b. recorders
   c. talking calculators

From *The Survival Guide for Kids with LD* by Rhoda Cummings, Ed.D., copyright © 2016. This page may be reproduced for individual, classroom, or small group use only. For other uses, contact Free Spirit Publishing Inc. at freespirit.com/permissions.

3. **Jayden understands math concepts really well. But he has trouble keeping the numbers lined up when doing subtraction and addition problems. Which type of assistive technology might help him?**

   a. optical character recognition systems
   b. personal FM listening systems
   c. electronic math worksheets

   Answers:
   1. b
   2. b
   3. c

Now you know about one way you can get help—through assistive technology. (Remember—talk to your parents if you think assistive technology can help you.) Keep reading to find out other ways to manage your LD and to get help.

From *The Survival Guide for Kids with LD* by Rhoda Cummings, Ed.D., copyright © 2016. This page may be reproduced for individual, classroom, or small group use only. For other uses, contact Free Spirit Publishing Inc. at freespirit.com/permissions.

Chapter 5

Ten Ways to Get Along Better in School

A lot of kids with LD do not like school. After all, it is not fun to have problems learning, especially when most of the other kids are not having problems. That may be why so many kids with LD get into trouble at school.

> "Sometimes I try to be real funny in class, but the teacher frowns."
> —Damien, 9
>
> "When I'm in trouble, I sit in a corner and look at my palms."
> —Tommy, 10
>
> "My teacher says I bother other kids. I'd rather talk than struggle with fractions."
> —Brianna, 11

Some kids with LD do like school. Maybe they do not like it all of the time, but they like it some of the time.

"The principal helps me with problems. My teacher reads with me and talks to me."
—Diego, 11

"I always go to the counselor so I can get out of class, but then she helps me."
—Kristy, 12

"I love art class. I do really good in art. Reading is hard but art is fun."
—Sindi, 10

If you do not like school, you can do something about it. There are ways to get along better in school. Here are 10 ways for you to try.

1. When Things Are Tough, Have a Chat

Often, kids with LD feel sad, hurt, and angry, but they do not share their feelings with others. They keep these feelings bottled up inside of them.

It is hard to keep feelings bottled up. Sooner or later, the feelings will come out. Sometimes they come out in strange ways. Some students with LD stop doing their schoolwork. Or they throw things, get into fights, or talk back to teachers. They get into trouble, and they feel even worse.

When you are feeling sad, hurt, or angry, talk to someone you trust. That person could be a school counselor, a teacher, a janitor, an aide, a bus driver, a relative, or a friend. Pick someone you like and trust, and who will understand you. Then tell that person about your feelings.

2. Keep Your Head Up!

Do not be ashamed of your LD. If someone asks you why you work with an LD specialist or why you get extra time to finish a test, tell them (if you feel like it). Look them in the eye and say, "I have LD." Or say, "I learn differently from other kids. The LD specialist helps me learn."

Believe and act like you are important. The more you do this, the more other people will treat you like an important person.

> I work with the LD specialist to help me learn. It's no big deal.

3. Become an Expert

An expert is someone who is the best at something. Kids with LD can become experts, just like anyone else.

Think of things that kids your age are interested in. What about singing or playing a musical instrument? Playing sports? Drawing or making art? Using apps and other technology? Knowing the latest songs and musical groups? Pick something you like that other students in your class like, too. Then find out as much as you can about it. Ask your teacher and your parents to help you.

This is a good way to show that kids with LD can be smart. It is also a good way to get attention. When you are an expert, other people will ask you for help.

4. Take Part in School Activities

School is more fun when you do things other than just schoolwork. So take part in school activities like plays, clubs, or sports. Offer to help plan school activities. Let your teachers know that you want to help.

Bennett

Bennett has LD. When he was in the sixth grade, he felt like he was not a part of the school. So he did not like going to school. His LD specialist suggested that he try out for the school play. He did—and he got a part! On the first night of the play, Bennett was nervous. But he did a great job! Other kids told him how good he was. Bennett felt like he found his place in school. He kept acting in more plays. Now he likes school.

5. Make Friends

Some kids with LD make friends only with each other. It is good to have friends with LD. But it is better to have friends who have LD *and* friends who do not.

In Chapter 7 of this book, you can read about some ways to make friends. If you want to read these now, turn to pages 63–71.

Kenny

Kenny was nine years old when he found out he had LD. He started working with an LD specialist. He made friends with other kids who had LD. But he also kept the friends he had before he found out he had LD. Now Kenny has lots of friends. He never feels alone or unpopular in any of his classes or in the cafeteria. Having lots of friends at school makes school more fun for Kenny.

6. Be a Helper

Many kids with LD feel like they are always asking for help. They feel like they are the only ones who ask for help.

But you don't just have to ask for help. You can be a helper, too! Maybe you can help younger kids who are learning things you already know. Or maybe you can help another student in your class with something you do well. If you know you can help, tell someone! Offer to help.

Helping others may make you feel more connected to your school. And then you will probably like school more.

7. Stay Out of Trouble

For many kids with LD, schoolwork is hard and boring. So they join in when other kids start goofing off. (After all, goofing off is more fun than working!)

This kind of joining in is not a good idea. It gets teachers and parents upset. If you see other kids goofing off, just ignore them. Keep doing your schoolwork. Then you will stay out of trouble.

Jessica

Jessica has LD. She was 10 years old when she learned to stay out of trouble. One day, the teacher was writing on the board. When she turned her back, the girls sitting on each side of Jessica made funny faces at each other. Jessica started making funny faces, too. The other girls stopped. But Jessica kept making faces. Just then, the teacher turned around and saw Jessica. She got in trouble and had to stay inside during recess that day. Jessica discovered that "fun" that gets you into trouble is no fun at all.

8. Know How to Relax and Cool Off

Think of the last time you were working on something very hard that you did not understand. Maybe you got frustrated. Maybe you got upset and angry.

What did you do next? Did you pretend to keep working when you were really not working? Did you yell? Throw your work on the floor? Quit? Cry? Go home?

These things will not help you get along better in school. You need to come up with other things to do instead.

Maybe you can raise your hand and ask your teacher for help. But what if your teacher is busy? Then you need to help yourself.

Here are ways you can help yourself:

- Close your eyes, take three deep breaths, and count to 10 very slowly and quietly.

- Say "relax" to yourself five times very slowly and quietly.

When you start to feel better, try doing your work again.

9. Do Not Use LD as an Excuse!

Some kids use LD as an excuse for not doing their schoolwork.

NEVER use LD as an excuse for not doing your work! It is your teacher's job to find the best ways to teach you. It is your job to work as hard as you can.

Even with the best teachers and the best books, some things will be hard for you. But NEVER use LD as an excuse for not trying. Doing this will not help you.

Amil

Amil is in middle school. Science is hard for him. When he has science homework, he often plays a video game instead. The next day, he tells his teacher he forgot to do his homework because he has LD.

Ava

Ava is in fourth grade. She does not like math. When the teacher asks students to work on math problems, Ava acts like she is trying hard. After a while, she stops. She goes to the teacher and says, "I have LD. These math problems are too hard for me."

10. Learn More About LD

Find out as much as you can about your kind of LD and the ways you learn. (You may want to read Chapter 2 again. It tells about the different kinds of LD.) When you have teachers who do not understand LD, you can tell them about it. This will help them plan for you. You can also tell your friends about your LD. This will help your friends understand you better. When people understand LD, they are often more patient with people who have LD.

Tips Just for Recess and the Playground

Most kids love recess. But kids with LD sometimes hate recess. They often get teased. They do not have anyone to play with. If you are one of these kids, try these tips to make recess more fun:

- Look for another kid who is alone. Think of a game the two of you can play. Then walk up to that kid. Ask if he or she wants to play the game with you. You will probably get a happy response. But be understanding if the kid wants to be alone.

- Join the group games, like tug-of-war, beanbag toss, jump rope, or kickball. Be brave. Go right up and get in line to play. Join as soon as you see the game start- ing. It might be harder to join if you wait too long.

Do you want to play catch?

- Pick the right kids to play with. Stay away from the kids who tease other kids and get into fights. Go up to the nice kids.

- Know the recess rules. That way, you will not get into trouble for breaking the rules. If you do not know the rules, ask your teacher.

- If you try these tips and still feel alone at recess, talk to your teacher or school counselor. Tell them how you feel about recess. Ask them for ideas for making recess better.

Tips Just for the Cafeteria

Like recess, lunchtime can be hard for kids with LD. Here are some tips for making lunchtime better:

- Try to have a lunchtime buddy—someone to get food with and sit with. Meet your buddy before going into the cafeteria. That way, you will not have to walk into the cafeteria alone. You will not have to search the cafeteria for your buddy.

- If you do not have a lunchtime buddy, look for another kid who is sitting alone. If that kid seems nice, ask if you can sit with him or her. That kid might be happy that you asked. Most people do not like to sit alone. Maybe that kid will become your lunchtime buddy.

- Plan ahead if you buy your lunch. Look at the weekly or monthly lunch menu. Circle what you will order each day. Planning ahead helps you move through the line faster. If you have trouble reading the menu, ask a parent, teacher, or friend for help.

● Talk to a teacher or school counselor if you have trouble carrying your tray. They can come up with a plan for helping you with your tray.

● If kids pick on you during lunch, sit near the lunchtime monitor. Kids are less likely to pick on others if an adult is nearby and they know they might get into trouble.

● If you try these tips and still find lunchtime difficult, talk to a teacher or school counselor. See if you can go to the library after finishing your lunch. That way—rather than sitting alone—you can spend your time reading or looking at books, listening to audiobooks, or quietly playing with apps on your phone.

How Will You Get Along?

This chapter gives a lot of advice for getting along better in school. Now it is time to think about that advice. The questions below will help you do that. You don't have to answer the questions right now. Just think about them and how you might answer them. You can also make a copy of this page to look at later. Or you can download and print out a copy at www.freespirit.com/LD.

- What difficulties do you have getting along in school?

- What advice do you think will help you? Why?

- What advice do you think will be the easiest to follow?

- What advice do you think will be the hardest to follow?

- What are some ways you might use the advice?

Thinking about the advice is not a one-day task. Keep thinking about the advice. Keep thinking about how you might use the advice. Then—when the time comes—use the advice that you think is right for you. You might find that the advice is very helpful.

From *The Survival Guide for Kids with LD* by Rhoda Cummings, Ed.D., copyright © 2016. This page may be reproduced for individual, classroom, or small group use only. For other uses, contact Free Spirit Publishing Inc. at freespirit.com/permissions.

Chapter 6

How to Get Along Better in School When You Get Older

Kids with LD in middle school and high school often have more trouble getting along. They feel extra stress. Or they have a harder time with other kids than they did in elementary school. They may feel more alone. This chapter gives advice for these important years.

Tips Just for Middle School

After six or seven years in elementary school, you are used to elementary school. You know where the classrooms are. You know most of the kids. You know what the rules are. Then you go into middle school.

Middle school is very different from elementary school. You have different teachers for different subjects. You go to different rooms for different classes. You have more homework. You meet new kids who went to different elementary schools.

Many kids—with or without LD—have trouble getting used to middle school. The following tips may help you adjust:

- Expect middle school to be different. If you expect a big change, it might not stress you out as much.

- Visit the school before classes start. Walk from classroom to classroom in the order that you will go to your classes so you get comfortable with the route. If you're going to have a locker, learn how to use it before school starts.

- Check with your friends about their class schedules. See if you have any classes together. Having friends in your classes will help you get used to the new routine.

- Have your parents talk to your teachers. Make sure your teachers know that you have LD. Talk with your teachers about the best ways for you to learn. Talk about whether assistive technology can help you. (See Chapter 4.)

- Once school starts, speak up if you are not getting the help that you need. As someone with LD, you have some special rights. For example, you have the right to sit at the front of the class if you need to. You also have the right to ask your teacher to give you homework that fits the way you learn best. (See Chapters 11 and 12 for more about your rights.)

- You will have a lot of homework to manage in middle school. So try to stay organized. Keep track of your assignments in a way that is best for you. Write them on a paper or electronic calendar, record them on an app that you speak into, or save them with a recording.

Tips Just for High School

High school is similar to middle school. You have different teachers for different subjects, and you go to different classrooms. Many of the tips that can help you adjust to middle school can also help you adjust to high school. But high school has its own difficulties. These tips will help you manage those difficulties:

- High schools usually offer more class options than middle schools. The number of options may feel overwhelming. So work with a parent or counselor when picking your class schedule. They can help you figure out what is best for you.

- Often, kids in high school are not supervised as much as kids in middle school and elementary school. There are often not as many hall monitors or cafeteria monitors. If you get bullied, talk to a teacher or school counselor. They can help you pick a new path to walk from class to class. They might even move your locker.

- You get more homework in high school. So remember to speak up to get the help you need.

- Join a club or other activity. Many kids in high school are very social. Kids who are not as social often feel even lonelier than they did in middle school. Try to make friends and find a way to belong to your school by joining a club or other school activity.

What Will You Do to Get Along Better?

This chapter gives lots of tips for getting along in middle school and high school. Look at the checklist below. Write what you will do on a separate sheet of paper. Or photocopy the checklist. Or you can download and print out a copy at www.freespirit.com/LD.

Check each tip that you will follow.

☐ I will expect a big change.

☐ I will find my classrooms before school starts.

☐ I will check with my friends to see if they are in my classes.

☐ I will have my parents make sure my teachers know that I have LD.

☐ I will speak up if I am not getting the help I need.

☐ I will stay organized with my homework.

☐ I will work with a parent or counselor to pick my classes.

☐ I will talk to a teacher or school counselor if I get bullied.

☐ I will join a club or other activity.

Keep this checklist. Refer to it when you feel like you are not getting along. Use the tips you checked to get along better. Think about using the ones you did not check. They may help you, too.

From *The Survival Guide for Kids with LD* by Rhoda Cummings, Ed.D., copyright © 2016. This page may be reproduced for individual, classroom, or small group use only. For other uses, contact Free Spirit Publishing Inc. at freespirit.com/permissions.

Chapter 7

Five Rules (and Tips!) for Making and Keeping Friends

Having friends makes school more fun. But it is not always easy to make friends. Kids with LD often have a tougher time making friends. But this does not mean you cannot do it! Kids with LD can have friends, just like everyone else.

There are social rules for making and keeping friends. These are different from other kinds of rules. You do not find them written down in books. Most kids learn the rules from other people as they grow up. But some kids with LD have trouble learning the social rules, just like they have trouble learning to read, spell, or do math. Here are some of the most important social rules (and some tips to help you follow the rules):

Social Rule #1:

Be Careful About What You Say

Some kids with LD often say exactly what they are thinking. Sometimes their words are hurtful. They may say,

"That shirt is ugly." Or they may say, "I don't like your haircut." They do not think about how their words might make someone else feel bad. But, of course, the other person is upset.

Social Tip #1:

Stop and Think

Saying hurtful things makes it hard to make and keep friends. So try to stop saying hurtful things. How? Do not blurt out what you are thinking. Instead, stop . . . and think about your words. Ask yourself, "Are my words hurtful?" If they are, do not say them.

Stopping and thinking helps in other ways, too. Before grabbing something that someone else has, stop . . . and think. Make sure the other person will not mind. Think about whether you should ask for the item rather than just grabbing it.

Zoey

Zoey was with her classmates on the playground. She liked Rania's winter hat. She ran up to Rania and grabbed her hat. Rania grabbed it back and then walked away. Zoey did not understand why Rania was upset.

Zoey needed to stop and think before grabbing Rania's hat. If she had done that, she might have realized that grabbing Rania's hat would upset Rania. Zoey might have realized that she should ask to see the hat. Zoey and Rania might have even started chatting about the hat. They might have become friends.

Social Rule #2:

Wait for Your Turn to Talk

Some kids with LD often interrupt when others are speaking. They do not mean to be rude. They simply do not know how to take turns in conversations. But other kids think it is rude. They do not want to be friends with someone who interrupts all the time.

Grace

Grace is 14 years old. She often walks up to kids and just starts talking. She talks even if another kid is already talking. The kids she walks up to often walk away from her. Grace does not understand why kids won't talk to her.

Social Tip #2:

Stop and Listen

To stop interrupting, you should stop . . . and listen. Do not say your words right away. Think about whether other people are talking. If so, wait. Listen for the right moment to say your words.

Also, listen to what is being said. Make sure to say things that are about the same topic. Do not start talking about something else. People do not like it when someone stops their conversation and starts talking about a whole new topic.

Social Rule #3:

Pay Attention to Nonverbal Signals

Nonverbal signals—or facial expressions and body language—tell a lot about what a person is feeling and thinking. So, in order to fully understand someone, you need to pay attention to the person's face and body movements. Paying attention to nonverbal signals will help keep you from insulting people, hurting people's feelings, and annoying people.

Social Tip #3:

Stop and Pay Attention

Understanding facial expressions and body language can be hard for kids with LD. To "read" these signals, stop . . . and pay attention. Pay attention to the person's face. Pay attention to how the person is standing or sitting. If you "read" the nonverbal signals, you will know how to adjust your behavior. Here are some of the most common nonverbal signals:

- Someone backs away from you. This means the person thinks you are standing too close. Do not move closer. Stay an arm's length away.

- Someone tenses up when you touch him or her. This means the person does not like being touched. Stop touching the person.

- Someone frowns. This means the person is unhappy. People may frown if you interrupt them, grab something from them, touch them, or do something else. Stop doing what is making the person frown. People may also frown if they are sad about something. If you think someone is sad, you can ask, "Are you okay?" This will show that you care about the person.

Manuel & Armando

Manuel and Armando are in the same class. They are good friends. They always high-five each other. One day, Armando was sad. His mother was in the hospital. Manuel went over to Armando. But Manuel did not notice that Armando was frowning and slumped in his chair. So Manuel smiled and tried to high-five him. Armando said, "Leave me alone!" This hurt Manuel's feelings. Manuel and Armando didn't talk for a while.

If Manual had "read" Armando's facial expression and body language, he could have asked Armando why he was upset. He could have used that moment to be a good friend to Armando—rather than losing his friend for a while.

Before talking to people, try to figure out how they are feeling. Are they smiling or frowning? Are they laughing and happy? Or do they sound angry? Are they busy with something and want to be left alone? Or do they seem like they are ready to talk? Figuring out how people are feeling can help you talk to them in the right way.

Social Rule #4:

Recognize a Mistake

Sometimes, people do things on purpose. They might bump into you on purpose. They might take your pencil on purpose. Other times, people do things by mistake. They bump into you. But they did not mean to. It was an accident. They take your pencil. But they did not take it to upset you. They simply thought you were done using it. Recognizing when someone does something by mistake can help you get along better with others.

Marcus is in fifth grade. He was sitting at his desk. Todd walked down the aisle. He bumped into Marcus by mistake. Todd started to say he was sorry. But Marcus stood up. He yelled at Todd. Todd again tried to say that he was sorry. But Marcus just kept yelling. Todd finally walked away.

Marcus

Social Tip #4:

Stop and Stay Calm

Do you have trouble recognizing whether someone did something on purpose or by mistake? If so, when something happens that upsets you, stop . . . and stay calm. If you do that, you might actually hear the person apologize. Then you will know that it was a mistake. You will know that there is no reason to get upset. If Marcus had stayed calm, he would have heard Todd apologizing. He would have known that Todd did not mean to bump into him. He and Todd might even have become friends.

If the person does not apologize, you should still stay calm. Tell the person that his or her action upsets you. Give the person a chance to apologize.

Social Rule #5:

Be a Good Friend

A friendship takes two people. Both people have to act like friends for the friendship to work. So one of the best ways to make friends is to be a good friend.

Social Tip #5:

Stop and Be a Good Friend

When you are around other kids, stop . . . and be a good friend. These tips will help you.

- Good friends ask about each other. They learn about their friends. So ask other kids questions about what they like to do. Or ask them about their favorite TV shows, sports, or music. Good friends share things about themselves. So after asking other kids about what they like, tell about the things you like.

- Good friends also encourage each other. So say nice things to other kids. Tell other kids when they did a good job on an art project or acting in a play.

- Good friends are kind to each other. So be friendly, share things, and do not tease. Treat other kids the way you want them to treat you.

- Good friends do not force friendship on each other. So do not try to *make* other kids be your friends, especially the most popular ones. You

might find good friends in students who are not popular. Is there someone who seems shy? Maybe that person is waiting for you to act friendly first.

Learning how to follow the social rules can be hard. It's worth it, though. Knowing and following the rules can help you make and keep friends. So practice at home with your family. Practice with your friends. Practice thinking before speaking. Practice listening and not interrupting. Practice paying attention to facial expressions and body language. Practice staying calm. Practice being a good friend!

Do You Know the Social Rules?

It's time for another quiz! (Remember, it's just for fun.) Answer the following questions. See if you know the social rules. Write your answers (just the letters) on a separate sheet of paper. Or photocopy the quiz to write on. Or you can download and print out a copy of the quiz at www.freespirit.com/LD. Check your answers at the end of the quiz.

1. **Your friend walks up to you. He is wearing new sneakers. You think they are ugly. What should you do?**
   a. Wait for your turn to talk.
   b. Look to see if your friend is frowning or smiling.
   c. Think about what to say so you do not hurt your friend's feelings.

2. **The kid next to you in class asks to borrow your marker. What should you do?**
   a. Yell at him for interrupting you.
   b. Let him borrow it if you don't need it.
   c. Move away from him as quickly as possible.

From *The Survival Guide for Kids with LD* by Rhoda Cummings, Ed.D., copyright © 2016. This page may be reproduced for individual, classroom, or small group use only. For other uses, contact Free Spirit Publishing Inc. at freespirit.com/permissions.

73

Quiz: Do You Know the Social Rules? (continued)

3. Someone steps on your foot when walking past you. What should you do?

a. Try to make the person become your friend.
b. Shove the person to show that you are angry.
c. Stay calm and think about whether the person did it by mistake.

Answers:
1. c
2. b
3. c

Knowing the social rules will help you get along better with people and make friends. So you might want to read this chapter again a few more times. Not today. But maybe in a week. And then in another week. Rereading the chapter may help you feel more comfortable with the social rules.

From *The Survival Guide for Kids with LD* by Rhoda Cummings, Ed.D., copyright © 2016. This page may be reproduced for individual, classroom, or small group use only. For other uses, contact Free Spirit Publishing Inc. at freespirit.com/permissions.

Chapter 8

How to Deal with Bullying

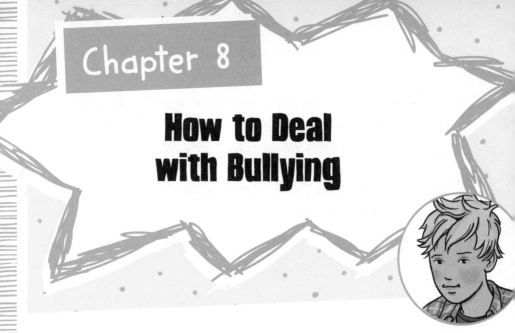

It is not right, but some kids bully other kids. Kids who bully often pick on kids who are smaller than them. Or who are less popular than them. They think that the kids they bully will not stand up for themselves. Many kids have probably been bullied at some point. Kids with LD are even more likely to be bullied.

Ahmed

Ahmed has LD. His speech is not always clear. Caleb noticed Ahmed's speech issues when they were in seventh grade. Caleb also noticed that Ahmed didn't have many friends. He started bullying Ahmed in the hallway. Caleb knocked Ahmed's books out of his arms. Sometimes he tripped Ahmed and called him names. Ahmed wondered if he would make it through seventh grade.

Teasing versus Bullying

Teasing is like joking. Teasing is not meant to hurt someone's feelings. Usually, it happens just once. If you love chocolate, a friend might tease you one day by saying, "You'd eat an ant if it were covered in chocolate!" The person who is teasing usually is smiling in a friendly way. The person who teases hopes that the other person gets the joke and laughs. Teasing can even make two friends closer.

Bullying is not like joking. Bullying *is* meant to hurt someone's feelings. The person who is bullying often has a mean look on his or her face. The person who is bullying tries again and again to make the other person feel bad. Someone who bullies might say something to you every day about chocolate to make you feel bad. "Hey, you'd eat a sock if it were covered in chocolate. You'd eat that old mop if it were covered in chocolate. You'd eat the school if it were covered in chocolate." They say these things to embarrass you. They say them to make you look weird to other kids. They say them to make you feel bad. That is bullying.

Four Types of Bullying

Bullying happens in different ways. No matter how it happens, it is hurtful and wrong. Here are four types of bullying.

Verbal bullying. The most common type of bullying is through words. People who verbally bully may say mean things about someone's clothes, hair, behavior, looks, or family. They may yell, whisper, or laugh as they bully.

Physical bullying. Kids who bully may also push and shove their targets (the kids they are bullying). They may kick, hit, or scratch them. They use physical power to hurt and scare others.

Relational bullying. This type of bullying can be hard to "see." It often happens through whispers behind the target's back. The person who is doing the bullying may spread lies and rumors about someone. Relational bullying also includes ignoring someone, leaving someone out of a group activity, and telling someone's secrets.

Cyberbullying. Sometimes kids use the Internet to bully. They may post mean or untrue things about someone on social networking sites. They may post embarrassing pictures just to hurt someone. They may "leave out" someone by getting other kids to not respond to that kid's posts. They may also send mean or threatening text messages to someone.

Kim

Kim has LD. She doesn't have many friends. But she is connected to many people on one of her social networking sites. One day, one of her Internet friends posted a bad story about her. The so-called friend said that Kim had stolen money from her teacher. This was a lie. The friend called Kim lots of bad names. Many of Kim's other Internet friends also began posting bad things about her. Then, they stopped replying to her posts. Finally, they dropped her from their own pages. Kim felt really sad.

Reasons Why Kids Bully

Kids bully for many reasons. Understanding why someone might bully may help you deal with your own hurt feelings when you are bullied.

Often, kids who bully are using behavior they see at home. Maybe one of their parents or an older sibling says and does hurtful things to other family members. So they act the same way.

Many kids who bully are often angry. They deal with their angry feelings by lashing out at others.

Kids who bully sometimes act that way because they are jealous of what other kids have. They may be jealous of someone's clothing or technology devices. They may be jealous that someone has true friendships with other kids. They may be jealous that someone gets along well with the teacher.

Sometimes, kids bully because they think that will make them popular. But often, the people who are their friends are just pretending. They pretend to be a friend because they don't want to be the target of the bullying.

Some kids who bully really don't want to bully. They are just following what another kid is doing. They don't want that kid to turn on them.

How to Handle Bullying

Getting someone to stop bullying you can be hard. These tips might work.

Stay calm. Kids who bully often enjoy stirring up emotions. So try not to get angry or look anxious. Instead, stand up straight. Look the bully in the eye. Then say in a calm voice, "I don't like that. Don't treat me that way." Even if the kid does not stop bullying you, you will feel good about standing up for yourself.

Walk away. If the kid keeps bullying you, do not say anything else. Just turn around and walk away.

Protect yourself. If the kid bullying you tries to hurt you physically, protect yourself. Cover your face with your arms. Lie face down on the ground. Yell for someone to help you. Try to run away. Safety should be your first concern.

Use the buddy system. People who bully often pick on targets who are alone. So try not to walk or sit by yourself. Buddy up with a friend—maybe someone else who is being bullied.

Talk to a trusted adult. You may feel like you are telling on the kid, but you are not. You are just keeping yourself safe. Tell what happened and who did it. The adult may have a way to stop the kid from bullying you without that kid ever knowing you said anything.

Repeat, repeat, repeat. Kids who bully can be strong-willed. They will often keep trying to bully you— even if you stand up for yourself. But keep standing up for yourself. Keep reporting the bullying. After a while, the kid may see that the bullying does not make you cry or feel bad about yourself. The kid may finally give up and leave you alone.

There are also things you should *not* do. You should not ignore the bullying. It will likely get worse if you ignore it. You should also not try to hit or threaten the kid who is bullying you. That will also make the problem worse. And you might get into trouble. Also, as hard as it may be, do not cry. That will only show that the bullying is working and the kid will keep bullying you.

And what should you do if you see someone else being bullied? Be an "upstander," not a bystander. A bystander stands by and watches. But an upstander helps by sticking up for a person in trouble. So stand up for the kid who is being bullied. After all, you would want that kid to do the same for you.

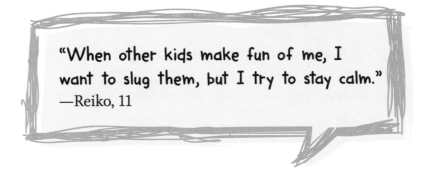

"When other kids make fun of me, I want to slug them, but I try to stay calm."
—Reiko, 11

How Will You Handle Bullying?

What will you do if you are bullied? Read the items below. On a separate sheet of paper, write down the tips you think you will use. Or photocopy the checklist. Or you can download and print out a copy at www.freespirit.com/LD.

Check all that apply on your list.

☐ I will stay calm.

☐ I will stand up for myself.

☐ I will walk away.

☐ I will protect myself.

☐ I will use the buddy system.

☐ I will talk to a trusted adult.

☐ I will stand up for other kids being bullied.

Think about what you checked. Why do you think those tips will work for you? Think about what you did not check. Why do you think those tips will not work for you? Is there any way you can make those tips work for you?

From *The Survival Guide for Kids with LD* by Rhoda Cummings, Ed.D., copyright © 2016. This page may be reproduced for individual, classroom, or small group use only. For other uses, contact Free Spirit Publishing Inc. at freespirit.com/permissions.

Chapter 9

How to Deal with Sad, Hurt, and Angry Feelings

Chapters 5, 6, 7, and 8 gave you tips for getting along in school, making friends, and dealing with bullying. Even so, you still may have sad, hurt, and angry feelings. This chapter will help you deal with those feelings.

Why Kids with LD Have These Feelings

Many kids with LD become unhappy. They do not think they are learning fast enough. Some of them have trouble getting along at school. Or they have trouble sitting still. Other kids laugh at the things they do and say. Then the kids with LD feel sad, hurt, and angry.

When kids feel sad, hurt, and angry, they sometimes say they do not want to go to school. Or they might make themselves sick. Some kids get mad at their parents, teachers, brothers, sisters, or other kids. Others get into trouble or stop trying to do their schoolwork.

"I guess I just want to know how come I can't be like everyone else and not be sad all the time."
—Eric, 13

"Kids laugh at me because I can't add numbers. I cry every day at school."
—Amy, 10

"Kids are mean to me. They call me names like stupid. My brothers tease me all the time because of the way I talk. I get mad because I have a problem. I don't like it. I wish I was like other kids."
—Finn, 11

Sometimes it seems that no one understands or cares what is happening. Other kids, teachers, or parents do not understand.

Alex

Alex has trouble with auditory processing (see Chapter 2). He cannot follow what his teacher is saying when she gives directions. He gets angry. He thinks no one understands him. Even when other kids try to be nice to him and help with the directions, he yells at them. He says, "Back off!" Or, "Leave me alone!"

Often, kids with LD do not know why they feel sad, hurt, and angry. The teacher or parent says, "Why did you throw that book?" The kid with LD says, "I don't know." He or she is telling the truth. It is hard for kids to explain why they feel the way they do.

When kids cannot tell someone about their sad, hurt, and angry feelings, the feelings do not go away. (This is true for everyone, not just kids.) So kids just keep feeling sad, hurt, and angry. It is hard for them to have fun. It is hard for them to do their schoolwork. It is hard for them to think about anything besides their feelings. We call this feeling depressed.

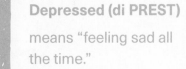

Depressed (di PREST) means "feeling sad all the time."

Six Ways to Help Yourself Feel Better

Do you ever feel depressed? Here are six things you can do to help yourself feel better.

1. Do some "I like me" exercises. If you exercise your arms, your arm muscles will get bigger. If you exercise the "I like me" part of your brain, it will get stronger.

Here are some "I like me" exercises you can try.

In the morning:

- Look in the mirror and think of five things you like about yourself. Say each thing out loud: "I like my _____."

- Find five ways you would like to do better. Say them out loud, too.

I like my hair. I like my singing voice. I like...

At night:

- Look in the mirror and tell yourself how well you did that day. Say: "Today I did better at

  _____."

Do these exercises each morning and each night until you feel better. If you like them, keep doing them.

2. Draw your feelings. If you have trouble talking about how you feel, try drawing pictures that show how you feel. For many kids with LD, this is easier than talking. You can show your pictures to a parent or another adult you trust.

3. Have a chat with a counselor. Many schools have counselors who are trained to help kids who feel depressed. Other counselors may work in offices near where you live.

You can tell your parents that you want to talk to a counselor. Your teacher or principal may be able to give you some names of counselors. Or your doctor can help you find a counselor.

Even if you are not sure what to say, counselors can often help you talk. You may need to see a counselor a number of times before you start to feel better.

> **Counselor (KOUN sel er)** means "someone who helps people by listening and giving advice."

4. Make a book about yourself. You can write a book about yourself. Or you can draw a book. Or you can make a book with both words and pictures.

Your book can have these parts:

Chapter 1: Things I Like Best About Myself

Chapter 2: Things I Would Like to Change
About Myself

Chapter 3: Things That Make Me Feel Happy

Chapter 4: Things That Make Me Feel Sad,
Hurt, or Angry

Chapter 5: How I Want to Be in 10 Years

5. Take life one day at a time. Do you sometimes think that you will NEVER get out of school? Do you worry about not having friends? Do you wonder if you will ever be independent?

Worrying about these things is normal. But worrying does not help. Try not to worry about the future. Instead, promise yourself every morning that you will do your best TODAY.

6. Be patient. When you are upset and want to give up, think about this: Many people with LD did not give up. Remember that you will not be in school forever. Remember that most of your teachers care about you and want you to learn. Most parents love their kids and want to help, too.

But most of all, remember that you are unique. No one else is like you. Look inside yourself and see all the good things. Do not take yourself too seriously. Learn to laugh at yourself. Be patient!

Dealing with Your Feelings

This chapter gives a lot of advice for dealing with your feelings. Now it is time to think about that advice. The questions below will help you do that. You don't have to answer the questions right now. Just think about how you might answer them. You can photocopy this page to look at later. Or you can download and print out a copy at www.freespirit.com/LD.

- Do you ever feel sad, hurt, or angry?

- Why do you think you have these feelings?

- How do these feelings make you act?

- What will you do to help yourself feel better?

Dealing with your feelings is an ongoing process. So keep asking yourself these questions. Keep figuring out ways to deal with your feelings. Because dealing with your feelings is an important part of being happy with yourself—and with getting along at school, with your family, and with your friends.

From *The Survival Guide for Kids with LD* by Rhoda Cummings, Ed.D., copyright © 2016. This page may be reproduced for individual, classroom, or small group use only. For other uses, contact Free Spirit Publishing Inc. at freespirit.com/permissions.

Ten Tips for Getting Along Better at Home

A big issue that some kids with LD face is that their parents do not understand what it is like to have LD. Parents sometimes do not understand the frustrations that kids with LD have. They sometimes do not understand that kids with LD try hard at school.

Maybe your parents have even told you, "We know you can do as well as other kids IF YOU WORK HARD."

Luciana is 11. One day after school, her dad tried to help her with her math homework. He kept explaining how to work the problems.
But no matter how hard she tried, Luciana couldn't complete any of the problems. Luciana's dad got frustrated. He said, "You aren't trying hard enough." This made Luciana feel bad. She threw down her pencil. She refused to finish her homework.

Luciana

Luciana's dad was trying to be helpful. But he did not understand that Luciana *was* trying hard. He did not understand what Luciana was feeling.

Sometimes parents are not the only ones who think that kids with LD just have to work harder. Sometimes teachers will say things like this to parents of kids with LD:

- "Your child would do fine if he was not so lazy."
- "Your child is smart enough. She just does not pay attention in class."
- "Your child could do good work if he cared more and acted up less."

Then parents tell the kids, "You are lazy." Or, "You do not pay attention in class." Or, "You do not care about school. You act up too much."

When this happens, kids get upset. If it happens to you, you probably get upset. No matter how hard you try in school, you still have a hard time at home!

Maybe it starts right after school. As soon as you get home, your mom or dad greets you at the door. They want you to do your homework RIGHT NOW! It seems like they never let up on you.

"My mom and dad feel good that I'm learning, but they want me to learn better. Sometimes they get mad at me when I don't understand what they want."
—John, 11

Why do your parents push you to do better all the time? They know you are not stupid. They want you to be the best you can be. They think that if you work harder, you will do better.

Maybe you and your parents get upset with each other. They yell at you. You yell back. What follows is one big fight.

But fighting does not help. Talking is better. And talking about your feelings is best. Tell your parents how you feel and how hard you work at school. Tell them you do not want to have a hard time at home.

Easy to say, right? Not so easy to do. It is hard to talk out loud about your feelings.

Here are some ideas to share with your parents. They are all ways to make things better at home. If you feel like you cannot talk to your parents, maybe you can show them this book. Ask them to read this section.

1. Tell Your Parents You Need Time to Relax

Most parents go to work. When they come home from work, sometimes they relax. They need a break before they do other work like paying bills or making dinner.

Going to school is your work. You need a break, too. Then you can start your homework.

Trevor

Trevor's mother always had him do his homework as soon as he got home from school. Sometimes, Trevor's mother would try to help him with his homework. But Trevor was always tired and had a hard time focusing on what his mother was saying. She would get upset. They would end up fighting. One day, Trevor told his mom that he was tired from school. He said that he needed a break when he got home. His mother understood. Now Trevor takes a break when he gets home. When he goes to do his homework, he isn't tired. He and his mother no longer fight when she tries to help him with his homework.

2. Tell Your Parents If Your Homework Takes Too Long

Homework may be good practice for you. And your parents probably think homework is important. Maybe they make sure you do your homework every night.

But do you feel that you are spending ALL of your time doing homework with NO time left over? Then your homework takes too long. To find out why, ask yourself these questions:

- Is it hard to understand what you are supposed to do?

- Is it hard for you to write neatly?

- Is it hard to keep the numbers lined up for math?

- Do the words get blurry (on paper or on screen) when you try to read?

- Are you tired from doing schoolwork all day?

Did you answer YES to any of these questions? Then tell your parents or teachers. Or ask your parents to talk to your teachers. Your parents should tell them how long it takes for you to do your homework.

You need time for yourself, too. Ask your parents and teachers if you can work out a plan. The plan should let you do homework and still have time left just for you.

3. Help Your Parents Understand Your LD

Sometimes parents do not know how hard it is to have LD. They get frustrated. So tell them how hard it is for you. Tell them how you feel when you do not understand something at school. Tell them how you feel when other kids do not understand you. Let your parents know that it frustrates you, too. Ask them to be patient. You may want to reread Chapter 2 with your parents. Chapter 2 tells about the different kinds of LD. Reading Chapter 2 may help your parents understand your LD better. That may help them be more patient.

4. Tell Your Parents Good News About Yourself

Sometimes parents are asked to come to school to hear about problems. Maybe their children are not doing their schoolwork. Maybe they are acting up. Maybe they are talking back to the teacher.

It is hard for parents to hear bad news. Some parents hear a lot more bad news than good news.

Tell your parents good news about you. Tell them the things you do right each day. Tell them when you are getting better at your schoolwork. Or when the teacher says something nice to you. Or when you make a new friend.

What if your parents are asked to come to school? They can ask to hear good things about you, not just problems. They also can tell the people at the school good things about you. Maybe your teachers think you are lazy or not trying. Maybe they do not understand you. Your parents can help. They can tell your teachers what you are really like.

5. Take Time Out When You Need It

Sometimes you may feel so upset that you just want to scream or run away and hide.

When you feel that way, take time out. Go for a walk. Go to your room, close the door, and listen to music. Ride your bike. Go fishing. Do something you like to do.

6. Make a Plan for Your Schoolwork

Do you have trouble remembering what schoolwork you should do at home? Make a list of the things you are supposed to do at home. Write on your list everything you need to bring home. Bring the list home, too. Make a check by each thing on your list after you do it.

Decide what time you will do your schoolwork. Right after you get home? After dinner? Pick a time when someone is there to help you if you need help.

Before you start your homework, find everything you need. Pencils, books, papers? What else? Turn off the TV and your music player. Do not text or call your friends. Perhaps you can even put a DO NOT DISTURB sign on your table. Then WORK!

7. Eat Well

Did you know that junk foods like soda, chips, and candy make it harder to think? Healthy foods like fruits and vegetables can help you think better.

If you need a snack, eat the good stuff. Skip the junk food. Do your brain a favor!

8. Get a Pet

If your parents agree, get a pet. When you feel angry, upset, or sad, you can talk to your pet. Your pet will never criticize you or make you feel bad about yourself. Also, it feels good to take care of a pet—your pet needs you! Your pet can be a dog, cat, bird, hamster, or goldfish.

9. Find a Hobby

Find something you like to do that gets your mind off school. Exercise. Play computer games. Listen to music. Make art. A hobby will give you something to talk about with other people. You may even become an expert. Remember that being an expert is a good way to show people how smart you are.

10. Get a Job

If you are old enough, and if your parents approve, get a job. Maybe you can babysit, get a paper route, or cut the neighbor's lawn. You could also collect cans and bottles and return them to the grocery store for the deposit money.

Getting a job may help you feel responsible and independent. It may boost your confidence. You may feel happier. You may get along better with your family. Getting a job may also help you think about what you want to do when you get out of school. You will also make some money that you can spend on your hobby!

What Will You Do?

The tips in this chapter may help you get along better at home. Which tips will you use?
Write them on a separate sheet of paper. Or photocopy this checklist. Or you can download and print out a copy at www.freespirit.com/LD.

Check the tips that you will use.

☐ I will tell my parents that I need time to relax.

☐ I will tell my parents that my homework takes too long.

☐ I will ask my parents to be patient.

☐ I will help my parents understand my LD.

☐ I will tell my parents good news about myself.

☐ I will take time out when I need it.

☐ I will make a plan for my time.

☐ I will eat well.

☐ I will get a job.

☐ I will find a hobby.

Sometimes it's hard to follow advice. You may forget about the advice. Or you may give in to a feeling of anger or frustration. So come back to your checklist on a regular basis. Reread it to remind yourself of ways to get along better at home.

From *The Survival Guide for Kids with LD* by Rhoda Cummings, Ed.D., copyright © 2016. This page may be reproduced for individual, classroom, or small group use only. For other uses, contact Free Spirit Publishing Inc. at freespirit.com/permissions.

Chapter 11

What About the Future?

Right now you might think, "I will never get out of school!" But you will be out of school and grown up before you know it. Maybe you think that once you are out of school, all your problems will be over. No more teachers on your back. No more nagging from your parents. You will be on your own. You can do what you want!

This is not the way it is. Being an adult is not easy. Doing just what you want can get you into trouble. When you become an adult, you must take care of yourself. You will also have to make decisions. One of the first decisions you will have to make is whether to go to school after high school or get a job.

That is a big decision. So you should discuss it with your parents and your guidance counselor. They can help you pick the right path for you. The following information will also help you pick the right path.

School After High School

Some kids with LD continue to go to school after high school. Some go to college—either a community college or a four-year college. Other kids go to a technical school or a vocational school. Talk to your parents and your guidance counselor about which path is right for you. Your guidance counselor can make sure you pick a school that provides support to students with LD. Here are some things you should know about each type of school:

Community college. A community college usually is a two-year college. The degree you receive when you graduate is called an associate's degree. Some jobs, such as administrative assistant or store supervisor, require only an associate's degree. But even if you want to get a degree from a four-year college, you might want to start at a community college. The campus is smaller. The classes are smaller. The smaller size will help you get used to being in college. Furthermore, most people who go to community college continue to live at home with their parents. So going to college feels less scary.

Sharla

Sharla has nonverbal LD. So she has a hard time "reading" people, but she is very artistic. She went to a community college so that she could live at home a bit longer. She got an associate's degree in graphic design. Now she works for an advertising agency. She lives in her own apartment.

After getting your associate's degree, you can apply to
a four-year college. But you likely will not have to complete all four years. You will get credit for many of the
classes you took at the community college. You will likely
just need to do two more years at the four-year college.

Four-year college. The degree you receive from a
four-year college is called a bachelor's degree. Many jobs
require a bachelor's degree. Many people who go to a
four-year college live on the college campus. Going to
college is a big change from life in high school. You have
to keep track of your own schedule, do your own laundry,
go to the store yourself to buy your shampoo, and do many
other things on your own. So starting at a community college can help you get used to what life is like in college.

Bernard

Bernard has reading LD. He went
to a college and got his bachelor's
degree in special education. Now
he teaches kids with LD in elementary school.

Technical school. A technical school is a lot like
community college. Many technical schools take two
years to complete. Technical schools also award an associate's degree. At a technical school, you will learn the
skills you need for a specific job in a technical field, such
as Web development, robotic engineering, or architec-
tural drafting. Some technical schools also offer degrees
in fields that many people do not think of as technical,

such as culinary arts (food) and home health care. Many community colleges also provide associate's degrees in technical fields.

Vocational/trade school. A vocational school teaches students the skills needed for a certain trade, like cosmetology (the skills needed to work in a hair salon). Vocational schools are also called trade schools. Other trades that can be learned at a vocational school include robotics, floral design, plumbing, and medical transcription. Depending on the trade, the time to complete a program at a vocational school can be 10 weeks to two years. Vocational schools usually award a certificate, not an associate's degree.

On the Job

Some kids with LD do not keep going to school after high school. Instead, they start working. If you decide to work and not go to school, be sure to get a job in a field that interests you. Then work hard at the job. If you work hard, you might get promoted. For example, let's say you start working at a restaurant as a server. You work hard and do a good job. You might get promoted to assistant manager. Then, you manage the other servers. If you work hard at that job, you might get promoted to restaurant manager. Then you'll help manage the whole restaurant, not just the servers. The more you are promoted, the more money you will make. But it takes hard work to be promoted. And it is not easy to work hard at something that you do not like. That is why it is important to get that first job in a field you like.

There are many jobs that require only a high school degree. Some of these jobs include a sales clerk at a store, delivery truck driver, security guard, and cable TV/Internet installer.

Marcus

After high school, Marcus went to work as a clerk at a supermarket. He loved talking to people and taking their groceries to their cars for them. He worked hard and was promoted to produce manager. He has worked there for nearly 20 years. This has been a great job for Marcus.

Your guidance counselor at school can tell you about more jobs that require only a high school diploma. Your guidance counselor can also help you pick the right job for you so that you will enjoy the job and work hard and be promoted. When choosing a job, you should think about whether you like to be outdoors or inside. You should also think about whether you like to work with other people or prefer to be left alone. Thinking about whether you like the same routine every day or prefer something new will also help you pick the right job.

You could also be an entrepreneur. That is someone who starts his or her own business. There are many possibilities for starting your own business. Do you love to cook? You could start a catering service that cooks food and takes it to other people. Do you like to clean? You could start a house cleaning business. Do you like dogs? You could start a dog walking business. Your guidance counselor and your parents can help you figure out if becoming an entrepreneur is right for you. So be sure to make an appointment with your guidance counselor before you graduate from high school.

Whether you decide to continue going to school or get a job, the following tips can help you succeed:

- **Ask for help.** You are learning how to do many things for yourself. But some things you will need help with. Do not be afraid to ask for help. You can ask your teachers, parents, friends, relatives, or other adults you trust.

- **Have a good work ethic.** Even if some things are hard for you, you should always keep trying to do your best and not give up. Never use your LD as an excuse for not doing your schoolwork or your work on the job. Always work hard and be proud of your efforts!

- **Have a positive attitude.** You will have good days and bad days. Everybody does! It is important not to get down on yourself. People like to be around others who are upbeat and positive. You are good at many things. Remember that you can learn, you just learn some things differently. Have confidence in yourself and tell yourself "I can do it!" (If you feel very down or sad, talk to your parents about getting help. You may also want to reread Chapter 9.)

- **Stay out of trouble.** School and work are not much fun if you are in trouble all of the time. You can learn to stay out of trouble. You can learn to stay away from other people who are up to no good. You can make positive choices.

- **Set goals.** It is easier to be successful when you know what you are working toward. Make a plan for what goals you want to reach. Decide what steps you need to take to help you reach your goals. Work hard and believe in yourself!

Your Life After High School

Do you have your plan for the future all figured out? No? Don't worry. Most kids don't. But think about the following questions. You don't have to answer them right now. But thinking about how you might answer these questions will help you plan your future. You can photocopy this page to look at later. Or you can download and print out a copy at www.freespirit.com/LD.

- Do you think you want to go to school after high school? What kind of school? Why?

- Do you think you would rather start working right away? Why?

- What kind of job do you want?

- What worries or fears do you have about the future? Who can you talk to about these worries?

- What makes you feel good about the future?

You probably cannot plan the best future for yourself by yourself. So talk to your parents and guidance counselor. Show them these questions. Talk about how you might answer them. These questions will help you have a good discussion with your parents and guidance counselor about your future.

From *The Survival Guide for Kids with LD* by Rhoda Cummings, Ed.D., copyright © 2016. This page may be reproduced for individual, classroom, or small group use only. For other uses, contact Free Spirit Publishing Inc. at freespirit.com/permissions.

Chapter 12

IDEA: A Law to Help Kids with LD Learn

Many years ago, kids with LD did not always get the help they needed at school. Many people—including teachers and principals—did not understand what LD was. But the parents of kids with LD wanted to help their children. They knew their children were smart and could learn. They wanted teachers and other people to think of ways to help their children.

All over the United States, parents began to talk to teachers and school principals. They began to work together. Parents of kids with LD worked with other parents whose kids had LD to make sure their kids could learn. They wanted schools to teach ALL kids—those with LD and also those with other problems. Because of their efforts, a new law called IDEA* was passed in 1975. The law has been updated many times since it was passed.

*The law was originally called Public Law 94-142 "The Education for All Handicapped Children Act of 1975." It was revised and changed to IDEA (Individuals with Disabilities Education Act) in 1990.

Important Parts of IDEA

Here are some important parts of IDEA:

- All kids, no matter what kind of LD or other kinds of challenges they have, must be allowed to go to school.

- All kids must be taught in the ways and classes that help them learn best. Schools must try to make the regular classroom the best place for kids with LD to learn. Kids with LD should only be taught in a different classroom if that is the best way for them to learn. An LD specialist must work with these kids to help them move back into the regular classroom.

- Schools must create a learning program for each kid with LD. The learning program explains the best way for the student to learn. The program must be written in a report called an Individualized Education Program (IEP).

- Schools must tell parents and students about the IEP. Parents have a right to ask for the IEP to be changed.

IEP means "Individualized Education Program" (in de VIJ oo līzd ej oo KĀ shen PRO gram)

This is a plan for one student. It tells what that student will learn that year and how he or she will learn it.

What the Law Means for Students with LD

The law means that kids with LD have a right to get the help they need. It says that students with LD should learn in the classroom that is best for them.

Many kids with LD learn best in the regular classroom. They do the same work as all the other kids. But they may receive some extra help from the teacher. They may also receive some extra help from an LD specialist who stays in the classroom.

Elena

Elena is in seventh grade. She has problems with writing. So Elena's teacher lets her say her answers out loud in class. She lets Elena record her homework. Elena can complete her work in the regular classroom. She just does it in a different way. Her way works in the regular classroom.

Khan

Khan is 10 years old. He sometimes has trouble understanding the words he reads. So during reading time, an LD specialist comes into the classroom. The specialist sits with Khan. He quietly works with Khan to help him understand what he is reading.

Other kids with LD need even more help in some subjects, such as reading or math. So they go to a different classroom. Sometimes this room is called a resource room. The students work with an LD specialist. They do the same work as the kids who stay in the regular classroom. But they get lots of help. They learn the subjects and do the work in a very different way. This is the best way for them to learn.

Tran

Tran is 10 years old. He is good at math, but he has trouble with reading. So he goes to a different classroom when his regular classroom does reading. He works with an LD specialist. He does the same reading work as the rest of the kids in his class. He just does it in a different way. He reads out loud. He also goes at a slower pace. So the way he does it would not work if he stayed in the regular class.

"Ms. Heinz is the best math teacher I ever had. She can break things down small enough for me to understand."
—Ricardo

Some kids with LD have trouble learning any subject in the regular classroom. They need to be in a smaller room. They need a quieter room. They need to have special ways to learn reading, math, and writing all day long. They may also have a hard time speaking or holding a pencil. So they do not go to the regular classroom for any subject. They spend the day learning in a different classroom called a self-contained classroom. It is also called the special education classroom.

Kendra

Kendra is the same age as Tran. When she talks, it is hard to understand her. She has trouble with all of her schoolwork. Because she needs more help than Tran, Kendra goes to a special classroom all day long. She gets special help with all her schoolwork. One day, she may go to some classes in a regular classroom. But for now, working in a special classroom is best for her.

LD specialists do more than just help kids with schoolwork. LD specialists help students listen and talk better, write better, even make friends more easily. As kids with LD learn to do these things, they can start spending less time with an LD teacher and more time in a regular classroom.

For many kids with LD, the LD room is a place where it is quieter and easier to pay attention. It is a place where it is always okay to have learning differences.

> "It is not bad to be in a resource room. Lots of my friends are in resource."
> —Aidan, 13

People with LD can learn many things, even if they must learn them in different ways. Some people with LD are very smart—even gifted!

This does not mean that school will be easy for you. It means that you can learn. How easy or how hard it will be depends on YOU and on your parents and teachers.

The good news is this: You are as smart as the other kids. You can learn what they can learn!

How Do You Learn Best?

Remember, IDEA says that your school must help you learn in the way that is best for you. So your school will work hard to come up with the best IEP—or learning program—for you. But you can have a say in your learning program. Read the questions below. Think about how you might answer them. Your answers will help you have a say in your learning program. You can photocopy this page to look at later. Or you can download and print out a copy at www.freespirit.com/LD.

- What kind of classroom are you in? Do you think this is the best way for you to learn? Why or why not?

- Do you think you need to spend more time working with an LD specialist? Why or why not?

- Do you think you would learn better if you were in a different classroom? Why or why not?

Do you think you need a different way to learn? Then talk to your parents. Have them talk to your teachers. Ask for help to find a different way to learn. Then you *can* learn!

From *The Survival Guide for Kids with LD* by Rhoda Cummings, Ed.D., copyright © 2016. This page may be reproduced for individual, classroom, or small group use only. For other uses, contact Free Spirit Publishing Inc. at freespirit.com/permissions.

Chapter 13

Getting into an LD Program

IDEA says that all kids, no matter what kind of problems they have, must be allowed to go to school. It says that all kids must be taught in the right kind of classes to help them learn.

This means kids with LD, as well as kids with other special needs, too.

Other Kinds of Kids with Special Needs

In addition to kids with LD, other kids with special needs get extra help or go to special classes at school.

Developmental disabilities. Kids with developmental disabilities are slow to learn, and they are not able to learn many things. This means that they have a very hard time in school and fall behind their peers. They also have trouble learning how to care for themselves. Some things they will never be able to learn. Many of these kids are in a special classroom for the whole day and not in a regular classroom.

Speech or language disability. This means having a hard time talking or understanding what other people are saying. Sometimes kids with this disability stutter or mix up sounds. It is hard for others to understand what they are saying. They are usually in a regular classroom but will leave to meet with a speech therapist.

Hearing or vision impairment. Kids with these kinds of problems have trouble hearing or seeing. Depending on how well they can hear or see, sometimes they are in the regular classroom. Some kids are not able to hear or see at all. Sometimes they go to a special school.

Emotional or behavioral disorder. This means having problems with the way one acts or feels. Kids with this problem act out and are often in trouble. They are sometimes mean and bossy to other kids and adults. They can get angry very easily.

How LD Is First Noticed

Students with LD need help with learning. But someone has to notice that a student has LD before that student can get any help. For each student with LD, it may happen a little differently.

When Reggie was nine years old, his mom took him to the doctor because he was having stomachaches. The doctor could not find anything wrong with Reggie. So the doctor talked with him. She asked Reggie if anything was wrong at school or home.

When Reggie said he did not like school, the doctor asked him some questions about schoolwork. She talked to Reggie's mom about what Reggie was like when he was younger.

The doctor thought Reggie might have LD. So she had his mom ask to have him tested for LD at school. Reggie was tested. The tests showed that he had LD. After Reggie began to get help from the LD teacher, his stomachaches went away.

Sheila

When Sheila was 10 years old, her dad read a story in a magazine about LD. He thought Sheila sounded like the kids in the story. He called Sheila's teacher to ask how he could find out if Sheila had LD. The teacher thought that Sheila was just slow to learn. But the teacher made sure Sheila got tested. It turned out that Sheila did have LD. So she got the reading help she needed in the resource room.

How Did You Get into an LD Program?

You read Reggie's story and Sheila's story. Different kids get into LD programs in different ways and for different reasons.

Are you in an LD program? Do you know how you got into the program? Here is how it might have happened.

First your teacher or your parents may have noticed that you were having a problem with learning. Your teacher and your parents talked to each other. Your teacher asked if some other people at your school could meet you and try to help.

If your parents agreed, then you probably were given some tests. Do you remember these tests? Perhaps you made shapes with blocks or copied shapes from cards. Maybe you repeated numbers or words. Maybe you put pictures in order to tell a story.

You also took tests in reading, spelling, and math. Maybe you listened to a story and then answered some questions about the story. Maybe you were asked to tell what certain words mean. You might have listened to sounds and tried to figure out what words they made.

Another person probably tested your ears to check your hearing, and your eyes to check your sight. Someone may have come into your class to watch you for a while to see how you follow directions, pay attention, and do your work. You may not have known that person was even there.

Your teacher and your parents also may have described where they thought you had trouble learning. They may have said how they think you learn best.

After these things were done, your teacher, the people who tested you, and your mom or dad got together to decide if you needed help because of LD.

If your teacher and the people who tested you thought you should have some special help, they met with your parents. At this meeting, everyone decided what you should learn and how you would be taught. Together they came up your IEP. (Remember, in Chapter 12, you learned that an IEP is an Individualized Education Program.)

Maybe all of these things happened with you. Or maybe your way of getting into an LD program went a bit different.

If you are in an LD program, your parents and teachers will discuss your IEP each year. The plan can then be updated to fit where you are in your learning. The law says that students with LD must be tested again every three years. This is to see if they still need help because of LD.

Maybe you did not think you were lucky when you found out you had LD. But many kids have problems with learning and never know why. They never get the help they need to succeed. So, in a way, you are lucky. You can get the right kind of help, so you can learn as much as possible.

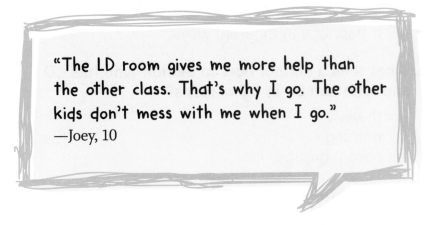

"The LD room gives me more help than the other class. That's why I go. The other kids don't mess with me when I go."
—Joey, 10

Getting Help for LD

Quiz

It's that time again—time for another quiz!
It's the last quiz of the book. (And once again, it's just for fun!) Write your answers (just the letters) on a separate sheet of paper. Or photocopy the quiz to write on. Or you can download and print out a copy at www.freespirit.com/LD. Check your answers at the end of the quiz.

1. How do adults notice that a kid has LD?

   a. Only by a kid having a stomachache.
   b. Only by a parent reading a story in a magazine.
   c. It happens in different ways.

2. What tells a school how to decide who has LD and who can be in LD classes?

   a. the law
   b. nothing
   c. parent groups

3. Which of the following is not a test for LD?

   a. repeating numbers
   b. copying shapes from cards
   c. running up and down the hallway

From *The Survival Guide for Kids with LD* by Rhoda Cummings, Ed.D., copyright © 2016. This page may be reproduced for individual, classroom, or small group use only. For other uses, contact Free Spirit Publishing Inc. at freespirit.com/permissions.

4. What is an IEP?

   a. a way of testing for LD
   b. an Individualized Education Program
   c. the name of the law that helps kids with LD

5. How often must students with LD be tested to see if they still need help?

   a. every three years
   b. every five years
   c. every ten years

Answers:
1. c
2. a
3. c
4. b
5. a

Remember, you have special rights as a kid with LD. Speak up for yourself. Make sure the law works for you. Make sure you get the help you need. After reading this book, you should know many ways to get the help you need. But if you need a reminder, just look at this book again. And then talk to your parents and teachers.

From *The Survival Guide for Kids with LD* by Rhoda Cummings, Ed.D., copyright © 2016. This page may be reproduced for individual, classroom, or small group use only. For other uses, contact Free Spirit Publishing Inc. at freespirit.com/permissions.

Chapter 14

A Happy Ending:
You Can Be a Winner!

You've learned a lot about LD—and yourself—by reading this book. The tips in this book can help you get along better now and in the future when you are an adult. Two people who followed a lot of the advice in this book are Cara and Jackson. They both have LD. They both are adults now, and they both have successful jobs that they love!

Cara

Cara has a hard time with spelling and reading. All through middle school and high school, Cara had to study very hard. But she is very bright. After high school, Cara went to a four-year college. Then she went to school for two more years to get a special degree.

Now Cara is a school counselor. She still has a hard time with spelling and reading. But she is working at a job she loves! Cara is a person with LD, and she is a winner.

Jackson

Jackson went to LD classes all through high school. He had trouble in reading and writing but enjoyed his high school computer classes. After he graduated from high school, Jackson went to a technical school and received an associate's degree in Web development.

Now Jackson works for a large company that develops websites for different kinds of businesses. Jackson has done his job so well that he is a supervisor in the company. He loves his job and looks forward to going to work every day.

Jackson still has a hard time reading and writing but is a whiz at Web development. Jackson is a person with LD, and he is a winner.

You can be a winner, too. There is no magic cure for LD. There is no pill, way of teaching, or diet that can make you not have LD. But having LD does not stop a person from doing great things and being happy and successful.

Now that you have read this book, you know there are ways to make things better at school and at home. Use these suggestions and remember:

You are a person with LD.

You are also a great kid.

You are a WINNER!

Resources for You

Do you want to know more about LD? Are you ready for more tips for getting along better? The following books and websites are good resources. Some of the books listed below are fiction. But reading about fictional characters can still help you understand LD and yourself better. Just as with this book, you may want to read the books and browse the websites listed below with a parent or teacher.*

*Parents and teachers: See the section on page 127 just for you.

Books for Kids with LD

The Alphabet War: A Story About Dyslexia by Diane Burton Robb (Morton Grove, IL: Albert Whitman & Company, 2004). Adam has dyslexia. Reading becomes a battle for him—and his teachers. But in third grade, he gets the help he needs. In fourth grade, he learns to love reading! (Fiction)

Fish in a Tree by Lynda Mullaly Hunt (New York: Nancy Paulsen Books, 2015). Ally is a whiz at math. But she has trouble with reading. She hid her LD all through elementary school. But when she gets to middle school, one of her teachers catches on—and gives Ally the help that she needs. (Fiction)

How I Learn: A Kid's Guide to Learning Disability by Brenda S. Miles and Colleen Patterson (Washington, D.C.: Magination Press, 2014). This guidebook provides an overview of learning disabilities and ways to learn better. (Guidebook for kids ages 9–12)

Niagara Falls, Or Does It? (A Hank Zipzer book) by Henry Winkler and Lin Oliver (New York: Grosset & Dunlap, 2003). The first in a book series about Hank Zipzer—the "world's greatest underachiever"—created by Henry Winkler of *Happy Days* (who had learning challenges himself). The series follows the everyday adventures of Hank, a bright fourth grader with learning difficulties. (The 2014 prequel series, Here's Hank, tells of Hank's adventures in second grade.) (Fiction)

Trout and Me by Susan Shreve (New York: Knopf Books for Young Readers, 2002). Eleven-year-old Ben has dyslexia and ADHD. He finds his first friend in Trout, another kid with learning disabilities. (Fiction)

Books for Teens with LD

365 Manners Kids Should Know by Sheryl Eberly (New York: Harmony, 2011). This guidebook provides instruction on proper manners for everything from opening doors for others to chewing gum to politely changing the subject. (How-To)

Bluefish by Pat Schmatz (Somerville, MA: Candlewick Press, 2011). Eighth-grader Travis cannot read. But at his new school, he is inspired to stop hiding his LD by an attentive teacher and a quirky girl. (Humorous Fiction)

Caged in Chaos: A Dyspraxic Guide to Breaking Free by Victoria Biggs (London, UK: Jessica Kingsley Publishers, 2005). Victoria Biggs wrote this book when she was 16 years old. Along with advice for how to get along better with dyspraxia—a type of LD that affects learning and motor skill development—the author describes her own problems with disorganization, clumsiness, and poor short-term memory. (Self-Help)

College Success for Students with Learning Disabilities by Cynthia Simpson and Vicky Spencer (Waco, TX: Prufrock Press, 2009). This guidebook offers advice for picking a college and preparing for life away from home, as well as tips for getting the help you need once you are at college. (Guidebook)

My Thirteenth Winter by Samantha Abeel (New York: Orchard, 2003). The author recounts how having dyscalculia, a type of LD related to math and numbers, caused her to have anxiety attacks and affected her self-esteem. (Memoir)

Please Stop Laughing at Me by Jodee Blanco (Avon, MA: Adams Media, 2003). In her best-selling memoir, Jodee Blanco tells the painful story of how she was bullied from elementary school through high school. (Memoir)

Please Stop Laughing at Us by Jodee Blanco (Dallas, TX: BenBella Books, 2007). In the follow-up to her best-selling memoir about being bullied, Jodee Banco offers advice to young people about how to respond to bullying. (Self-Help)

A Note to Parents and Teachers

If you've read this book, then you've taken a great step toward better understanding your children or students with LD. (And if you're just peeking at the resources, you may find it helpful to read the whole book. It's written for young people. But it can give you great insight into the daily struggles that kids with LD face.) This book will also help you better understand LD, give you tips for helping your children or students manage their LD, and help you understand how the law IDEA is supposed to work for them.

You may also want to read the following books and websites. They will give you more information about LD as well as ways to help your kids learn. If you're looking for even more information, you may want to contact one of the organizations listed at the end of this section.

Books

Bridging the Gap: Raising a Child with Nonverbal Learning Disorders by Rondalyn Varney Whitney, MOT, OTR (New York: The Berkeley Publishing Group, 2002). The author structures her guidebook for raising children with nonverbal LD around her own experiences raising her son. (Guidebook/Memoir)

Classrooms That Work: They Can All Read and Write by Patricia M. Cunningham and Richard L. Allington (London, UK: Pearson, 2015). The authors provide strategies for literacy instruction that is inclusive of a variety of learning styles and difficulties. (Guidebook)

How Language Works: How Babies Babble, Words Change Meaning, and Languages Live or Die by David Crystal (New York: Avery, 2007). Understanding how language works and how the brain processes information can help parents and teachers of children with problems with language better understand and help them. (Nonfiction/Language Arts)

It's So Much Work to Be Your Friend: Helping the Child with Learning Disabilities Find Social Success by Richard Lavoie (New York: Touchstone, 2005). After explaining why children with LD have problems with making and keeping friends, the author provides extensive advice for helping your kids navigate the social world. (Guidebook)

The Misunderstood Child: Understanding and Coping with Your Child's Learning Disabilities by Larry B. Silver, M.D. (New York: Three Rivers Press, 2006). This classic guidebook includes lots of information related to what causes and how to deal with the problems that are often associated with LD, such as depression and anger. It also includes a detailed section on the evaluation process for identifying children with LD. (Guidebook)

A Parent's Guide to Special Education: Insider Advice on How to Navigate the System and Help Your Child Succeed by Linda Wilmshurst, Ph.D., and Alan W. Brue, Ph.D., NCSP (New York: AMACOM, 2005). This book provides step-by-step guidelines for getting your child into a special education program and how to help manage his or her education once in the program. (Guidebook)

Raising Resilient Children by Robert Brooks, Ph.D., and Sam Goldstein, Ph.D. (New York: McGraw-Hill Education, 2002). This guidebook goes into great detail about a variety of ways to help your children with LD overcome issues with poor self-esteem and develop a high sense of self-worth. (Guidebook)

Thinking Differently: An Inspiring Guide for Parents of Children with Learning Disabilities by David Flink (New York: William Morrow Paperbacks, 2014). Flick provides great detail about the legal rights of children with LD in a way that is accessible to those not familiar with legal terms. The author also provides a wealth of information for advocating for your child at school. (Guidebook)

Websites

Bookshare (www.bookshare.org) A free online library of audiobooks that houses over 300,000 titles for people with print disabilities.

GreatSchools/GreatKids (www.greatschools.org/gk) This website has a section devoted to advice, advocacy, and research related to learning disabilities.

Building the Legacy: IDEA 2004 (idea.ed.gov) Designed to answer questions about the Individuals with Disabilities Education Act, this site works in partnership with service providers, administrators, families and advocates, and policymakers to support efforts to help all children learn and progress.

LD Online (www.ldonline.org) Contains a wealth of information related to learning disabilities, including ways to teach kids with LD, finding help for kids with LD, and the latest research about LD.

Learning Ally (www.learningally.org) The nonprofit organization works with parents and educators to help dyslexic and visually impaired students learn better; fee-paying members can access audio textbooks and other literature through their website.

Reading Rockets (www.readingrockets.org) Devoted to providing young readers with the tools they need to succeed at reading, this site features a section on assistive technology for students with LD as well as sections on understanding why some students struggle with reading and how to get help for them.

Understood for Learning and Attention Issues (www.under stood.org) This site provides information for getting the help you need from schools as well as tips for managing challenges with friends and family.

Organizations

Council for Learning Disabilities (CLD)
(913) 491-1011 • www.council-for-learning-disabilities.org
CLD is an international organization committed to empowering people with learning disabilities at all stages in their life by enhancing their opportunities for education and improving their quality of life.

Learning Disabilities Association of America (LDA)
(412) 341-1515 • www.ldanatl.org
Members of LDA include professionals and parents devoted to advancing the education and well-being of children and adults with learning differences. Visit their website for information on state and local chapters.

National Center for Learning Disabilities (NCLD)
(888) 575-7373 • www.ncld.org
NCLD provides national leadership in support of children and adults with learning disabilities. They offer referral services, develop and advocate for educational programs, and promote public awareness.

Index

A

Activities, 4–5
  about your life after high school, 106
  assistive technology quiz, 44–45
  bullying quiz, 80
  checklist about getting along better at home, 98
  checklist about middle and high school, 62
  for determining your type of learning difference, 29–30
  on feelings, dealing with, 88
  on finding out about yourself, 14–15
  getting along in school quiz, 57
  on getting into LD program, 120–121
  helping you determine how you learn best, 113
  on how your brain works, 35–37
  social rules quiz, 72–73
Adults. *See* Parents; Teachers
Adult, talking to a trusted
  about this book, 3
  about your feelings, 47–48, 85
  bullying and, 78
Alternative keyboards, 39–40
Apologies, 69
Assistive technology
  alternative keyboards, 39–40
  audiobooks, 39
  electronic math worksheets, 42
  explained, 38–39
  in middle school, 60
  optical character recognition systems, 39
  personal FM listening systems, 41–42
  recorders, 41
  speech recognition programs, 40
Associate's degree, 100–101
Attention deficit hyperactivity disorder (ADHD), 26
Attitude, positive, 105
Audiobooks, 39

Auditory processing disorders
  feelings and, 82
  personal FM listening systems for, 41–42
  understanding what others are saying, problems with, 23–25
  understanding what you hear, problems with, 22–23

B

Bachelor's degree, 101
Behavioral disorders, 115
Body language, reading and paying attention to, 66, 67–68
Book(s)
  audio, 39
  for kids with learning differences, 124–125
  made about yourself, 85–86
  for teens with learning differences, 125–126
Bookshare (website), 128
Brain
  differences in processing of information in, 11
  how information gets to, 31
  organization of signals received to, 32–33
  receiving signals, problems with, 31–32
  sending out signals, problems with, 33
Buddy system, 78
Building the Legacy: IDEA 2004 (website), 128–129
Bullying
  cyberbullying, 76
  ignoring, 79
  physical, 76
  quiz on, 80
  reasons for, 77
  relational, 76

standing up for someone else
experiencing, 79
teasing vs., 75
tips for handling, 77–79
verbal, 75
Business, starting your own, 104

C
Calculators, talking, 42
Calm, staying, 69, 77–78
Cell phones
recording assignment instructions on,
21, 39
speech recognition programs and, 40
Classroom
IDEA on kids with LDs in a regular,
108
LD students going to a different, 110,
111
LD students learning in the regular,
109
sitting in the front of, 60
for students with developmental
disabilities, 114–115
Clubs, high school, 61
College, 100–101, 122
Communicating with others
about bullying, 78
about your feelings, 47–48, 85, 91
not interrupting and, 65–66
thinking about what is said, 63–65
with your parents, 91–95
Communication, parent-teacher.
See Teachers, parents
communicating with
Community colleges, 100
Computers
alternative keyboards for, 39–40
audiobooks downloaded to, 39
electronic math worksheets and, 42
learning to write using, 18
recording assignment instructions on,
21
speech recognition programs and, 40
Confidence in yourself, 105
Council for Learning Disabilities, 129
Counselors, 85. See also Guidance
counselors
Culinary arts (food), 101–102
Cyberbullying, 76

D
Depressed, feeling, 83, 84–87
Developmental disabilities, 114–115
Drawing your feelings, 85
Dyscalculia. See Math, problems with
(dyscalculia)

Dysgraphia. See Writing, problems with
(dysgraphia)
Dyslexia. See Reading, problems with
(dyslexia)

E
Eating habits, 96
Electronic math worksheets, 42
Emotional disorders, 115
Emotions. See Feelings
Employment, 97, 103–105
Entrepreneurs, 104
Executive functioning, problems with,
26–27
Expertise, gaining, 49, 97

F
Facial expressions, reading, 26, 67–68
Facial expressions, reading and paying
attention to, 66
Feelings
advice on helping yourself feel
better, 84–87
from being depressed, 83
drawing your, 85
impact of sad, hurt, and angry, 81–82
not understanding your, 83
student quotes about, 83
talking to someone about your, 47–48
Finger grip, 19
Fingers, used for solving math
problems, 20
Flash cards, 20
Food, eating healthy, 96
Four-year colleges, 101
Friendships. See also Social rules
being a good friend and, 70–71
getting along at school and, 50
middle school classes and, 59
Frowning, 67

G
Genetics, learning differences and, 11
Goals, setting, 105
GreatSchools/GreatKids (website), 128
Guidance counselors, 99, 100, 104, 106

H
Healthy foods, 96
Hearing impairments, 115
Hear, problems with understanding
what you, 22–23, 30–31
Helping out at school, 50–51
High school, 60–61
continuing with school after,
100–102, 104–105

Hobbies, 97
Home health care, 102
Homework
    in high school, 61
    making a plan for completing, 95–96
    in middle school, 60
    relaxing before working on, 91, 92
    spending too much time on, 92–93
    talking to parents about, 93
    tips for visual perceptual/visual
        motor deficits, 22

I

IDEA (Individuals with Disabilities
        Education Act) (1990),
        107–113, 114
    activity on, 113
    important parts of, 108
    meaning of, for students with
        learning differences, 109–112
    passage of, 107
    personal stories about, 110, 111
IEPs (Individualized Education
        Program), 108, 119
"I like me" exercises, 84–85
Instructions
    asking for written, 23, 34
    recorded, 21, 41
Interrupting others, 65, 66

J

Jobs, 97, 103–105
Junk food, 96

L

Language disabilities, 115
Language processing disorder, 23–25
LD. See Learning difference(s)
LD Online (website), 129
LD programs, getting into
    activity on, 120–121
    decisions about your IEP and, 118–119
    noticing LD differences in student
        and, 115–116
    testing and, 117–118
LD specialists
    assistive technology and, 42–43
    Individuals with Disabilities Educa-
        tion Act (IDEA) and, 108, 109
    roles of, 112
    students seeing in a different
        classroom, 110
    talking to, 34
Learning Ally (website), 129
Learning difference(s)
    the brain and, 31–34

causes of, 11–12
explained, 7
identifying students with, 12–13, 116
not being ashamed of your, 48
not using as an excuse for doing
        work, 104–105
problems associated with, 26–27
Learning differences, students with. See
        also Personal stories
    approaches to learning differently, 34
    becoming experts at something,
        49, 97
    books for, 124–126
    characteristics describing, 1, 30–31
    characteristics not describing, 10–11
    differences among, 8–9
    learning more about their LD, 53–54
    six great gripes of, 6
    taking time out for themselves, 95
Learning differences, types of, 16–27
    auditory processing disorder (under-
        standing what is heard), 22–23
    dyscalculia (math problems), 19–20
    dysgraphia (writing problems), 17–19
    dyslexia (reading problems), 16–17
    nonverbal skills, problems with,
        25–26
    understanding language, problems
        with, 23–25
    visual perceptual/visual motor deficit
        (understanding what is seen),
        20–21
Learning Disabilities Association of
        America (LDA), 129
Learning disability, learning
        differences vs., 7
Library (school), 56
Listening to others, 65–66
Lockers, school, 59
Lunch menus, 55–56
Lunchtime, 55–56
Lunchtime buddy, 55

M

Math facts, memorizing, 20
Math, problems with (dyscalculia),
        19–20
    electronic math worksheets for, 42
    learning methods for students with, 34
    talking calculators for, 42
Memory, 26–27
Middle school, 58–60
Mistakes by others, recognizing, 68–69
Multiplication tables, 19
Muscles, lack of control over, 25–26

N

National Center for Learning
Disabilities (NCLD), 129
Nonverbal learning disabilities, 25–26
Nonverbal signals, reading and paying
attention to, 66–68

O

Optical character recognition systems, 39
Organizations, 129
Organization skills, 27, 60

P

Parents. *See also* Teachers, parents
communicating with
arguments with, 90
assistive technology and, 42–43
books for, 127–128
getting into an LD program and,
117–118
homework and, 92–93
IDEA and, 107
lack of understanding by, 89–90
noticing LDs in their child, 116
organizations for, 129
people considered as your, 3
pushing you to work harder, 90–91
talking to, about good news about
yourself, 94
talking to, about your homework,
92–93
talking to, about your learning
disabilities, 93–94
talking to, about your need to relax,
91–92
websites for, 128–129
Patience, 87
Pen/pencil, correct way of holding, 18–19
Personal FM listening systems, 41–42
Personal stories, 4
on accepting apologies, 69
on bullying, 74
on differences among kids with
learning differences, 9
on feelings of sadness and anger, 82
on friendships, 50, 68
on getting along with parents, 89, 90,
92
on LD students learning in a
different classroom, 111
on LD students learning in a regular
classroom, 109
on life after high school, 100, 101
on math problems, 19
on problems related to understand-
ing/processing language, 24

on problems related to understanding
what is heard, 23, 32
on problems relating to understanding what is seen, 21
on problems with nonverbal skills, 25
on reading problems, 17
on speech recognition program, 40
on staying out of trouble at school, 51
on students learning in a different
classroom, 110
on successful adults with LDs, 122–123
on taking part in school activities, 49
on thinking about what you say, 64
on using your LD as an excuse for not
working hard, 53
on working after high school, 103
on writing problems, 18
Pets, 96
Physical bullying, 76
Playground time, 54–55
Positive attitude, 105
Public Law 94-142, 107

Q

Quizzes
on assistive technology, 44–45
on getting help for LD, 120–121
on how your brain works, 35–37
on social rules, 72–73

R

Reading out loud, 17, 34
Reading, problems with (dyslexia), 16–17
audiobooks and, 39
learning strategies for students with, 34
optical character recognition
systems for, 39
Reading Rockets (website), 129
Recess, 54–55
Recorded instructions, 21, 41
Recorders, 41
Recordings of a text, 39
Relational bullying, 76
Relationships. *See also* Friendships;
Parents; Social rules
lunchtime at school and, 55–56
recess and, 54–55
Relaxation methods, 52
Remembering things, problems with,
26–27
Resource room, 110
Rights, for students with learning
differences, 60. *See also* IDEA
(Individuals with Disabilities
Education Act) (1990)
middle school and, 60
Ruler, used for reading, 17, 34

S

School
becoming an expert at something in, 49
bullying at. *See* Bullying
helping out at, 50–51
high school, tips for, 60–61
liking/not liking, 46–47
lunchtime at, 55–56
middle school, tips for, 58–60
not being ashamed of your LD at, 48
not using your LD as an excuse at, 52–53
options for life after high school, 99–105
quiz on getting along at, 57
recess/playground time at, 54–55
relaxing at, 52
special needs students in, 114–115
staying out of trouble at, 51
taking part in activities at, 49, 61
talking about your emotions to a trusted person at, 47–48
talking to others about your LD at, 53–54
tips for succeeding in life after, 104–105
Self-contained classroom, 111
Signals, brain, 31–33
Social rules
activity on, 72–73
being a good friend and, 70–71
not interrupting others, 65–66
paying attention to nonverbal signals, 66–68
recognizing mistakes by others and, 68–69
thinking about you say, 63–65
Special education classroom, 111
Special needs students, 114–115
Speech disabilities, 115
Speech recognition programs, 40
Subtraction, 19

T

Talking calculators, 42
Teachers. *See also* LD specialists
books for, 127–128
getting into an LD program and, 117, 118
lack of understanding by, 90
middle school, communicating with, 60
organizations for, 129

websites for, 128–129
writing down assignments, 23, 34
Teachers, parents communicating with
about assistive technology, 42–43, 60
about schoolwork, 90, 93
about written instructions, 23
about your strengths, 94
getting into an LD program and, 117–118
middle school teachers, 60
Teasing
bullying *vs.*, 75
friendships and, 70
at lunchtime, 56
at recess, 54
Technical schools, 100, 101–102
Tests/testing
asking teachers for more time for, 34, 48
identifying learning differences (LDs) and, 13, 116, 117
law requiring, every 3 years, 119
Time, keeping track of, 27
Trade schools, 102
Two-year colleges, 100–101

U

Understood for Learning and Attention Issues (website), 129

V

Verbal bullying, 75
Vision impairments, 115
Visual perceptual/visual motor deficit, 20–21
Vocational schools, 100, 102

W

Websites, 128–129
Worrying, 87
Writing movements, practicing, 18
Writing, problems with (dysgraphia), 17–19
alternative keyboards for, 39–40
learning methods, 34
recorders for, 41
speech recognition programs for, 40
Written instructions, 23

Z

Zen doodling, 18

About the Author

Rhoda Cummings, Ed.D., is professor emeritus of counseling and educational psychology at the University of Nevada, Reno. She has two grown children: Carter, who has LD, and Courtney Elizabeth. For over 30 years, Rhoda has worked with kids with LD, parents, and college students studying to be special education teachers.

Rhoda has written a number of books about learning disabilities, including *Parenting the Learning Disabled: A Practical Handbook* and *Career and Vocational Education for the Mildly Handicapped*. With her friend and colleague, Gary Fisher, she coauthored the original *Survival Guide for Kids with LD*. She also has written a college textbook on adolescent development, *Adolescence: A Developmental Perspective*.

Rhoda lives on the beautiful Oregon Coast and spends her time reading, writing, and painting.

Other Great Books from Free Spirit

The Survival Guide for Making and Being Friends
James J. Crist, Ph.D.
For ages 8–13.

The Survival Guide for Kids with Behavior Challenges
Tom McIntyre, Ph.D.
For ages 9–14.

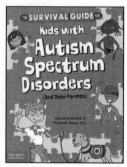

The Survival Guide for Kids with Autism Spectrum Disorders (And Their Parents)
Elizabeth Verdick and Elizabeth Reeve, M.D.
For ages 9–13.

The Survival Guide for Kids with ADHD
John F. Taylor, Ph.D.
For ages 8–12.

The Survival Guide for Gifted Kids
Judy Galbraith
For ages 10 & under.

The Survival Guide for School Success
Ron Shumsky, Susan M. Islascox, and Rob Bell
For ages 10–14.

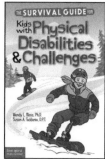

The Survival Guide for Kids with Physical Disabilities & Challenges
Wendy L. Moss, Ph.D., and Susan A. Taddonio, D.P.T.
For ages 8–13.

Find all the Free Spirit SURVIVAL GUIDES for Kids
at www.freespirit.com/survival-guides-for-kids

Interested in purchasing multiple quantities and receiving volume discounts?
Contact edsales@freespirit.com or call 1.800.735.7323 and ask for Education Sales.

Many Free Spirit authors are available for speaking engagements, workshops, and keynotes. Contact speakers@freespirit.com or call 1.800.735.7323.

For pricing information, to place an order, or to request a free catalog, contact:

Free Spirit Publishing Inc.
6325 Sandburg Road • Suite 100 • Golden Valley, MN 55427-3674 • toll-free 800.735.7323
local 612.338.2068 • fax 612.337.5050 • help4kids@freespirit.com • www.freespirit.com